101

solution-focused questions
for help with <u>trauma</u>

THE 101 SOLUTION-FOCUSED QUESTIONS
SERIES OF BOOKS BY
FREDRIKE BANNINK

101 Solution-Focused Questions for Help with Anxiety

101 Solution-Focused Questions for Help with Depression

101 Solution-Focused Questions for Help with Trauma

Books available
separately or as a set.

A NORTON PROFESSIONAL BOOK

101

solution-focused questions for help with trauma

FREDRIKE BANNINK

W.W. Norton & Company

New York | London

For information about permission to reproduce selections from this book,
write to Permissions, W. W. Norton & Company, Inc.,
500 Fifth Avenue, New York, NY 10110

For information about special discounts for bulk purchases, please contact
W. W. Norton Special Sales at specialsales@wwnorton.com or 800-233-4830

Manufacturing by RR Donnelley Westford
Book design by Molly Heron
Production manager: Christine Critelli

Library of Congress Cataloging-in-Publication Data

Bannink, Fredrike.
101 solution-focused questions for help with trauma / Fredrike Bannink.
—First edition.
pages cm.—(A Norton professional book)
Includes bibliographical references and index.
ISBN 978-0-393-71112-7 (pbk.)
1. Post-traumatic stress disorder—Treatment—Miscellanea.
2.Solution-focused brief therapy. I. Title. II. Title: One hundred one
solution-focused questions for help with trauma. III. Title: One hundred
and one solution-focused questions for help with trauma.
RC552.P67B334 2015
616.85'21—dc23

2015023989

W. W. Norton & Company, Inc.
500 Fifth Avenue, New York, N.Y. 10110
www.wwnorton.com

W. W. Norton & Company Ltd.
Castle House, 75/76 Wells Street, London W1T 3QT

1 2 3 4 5 6 7 8 9 0

"I am not what happened to me.
I am what I choose to become."

———————

Jung's (1965) quote
will be the theme
of this book.

Christina the Astonishing
Patron Saint of Insanity and Lunatics

I am from Belgium. I am remembered for my faith and for my violent fits of ecstasy. I died but came back to life. Psalm 102 is attributed to me. It is the prayer of the afflicted:

> For my days vanish like smoke
> I am like an owl in the desert among the ruins
> I have mingled my drink with weeping
> And my days are like a shadow
> Pray for me

Contents

Acknowledgments

According to Steve De Shazer, one of the founders of solution-focused brief therapy, differences in and of themselves are just differences. But some people (and some animals) have made a difference that has been significant in my life and my work. In one way or another, they all assisted me in writing these volumes.

I thank my colleagues, students, and above all my clients, who have helped me discover, apply, and improve my work over the years. I thank my publisher, Deborah Malmud, for her invitation to write these volumes; my friend and colleague Suzanne Aldis Routh for translating; and my colleague Kaz de Jong for reviewing this book.

To my husband, I am grateful for your continuing love and support. To my four Italian cats, *mille grazie* for keeping me company during the many pleasant hours of writing.

101

solution-focused questions
for help with trauma

Introduction

This is a book to help clients use what happened to them to make their lives *better instead of bitter*. In psychotherapy with trauma survivors, there can be a range of outcomes. For some, there is full or partial recovery from symptoms of PTSD, and that is as far as these clients can go. For others, there is not only recovery from symptoms but also posttraumatic growth. For some people, the outcome involves finding a resiliency that allows them to go on with their lives.

This book aims to help clients struggling with trauma by being first and foremost a practical book aimed at all professionals working with trauma survivors, offering them solution-focused (SF) viewpoints and skills. The book invites them to change their focus from what is wrong to what is right with their clients and from what isn't working to what is working in their lives.

Traditional psychotherapy has been strongly influenced by the medi-

cal model.[1] The structure of problem-solving—first determining the nature
of the problem and then intervening to minimize suffering—influences
the content of the interaction between therapists and clients; the focus is
on pathology. However, it is not this negative way of thinking but clients'
strengths, competencies, and resources that are most important in bringing
about positive change. The secret of change is to focus all energy not on
fighting the old, but on building the new.

This is Volume 3 of a series of three books, each offering 101 solution-focused questions for help with a specific psychiatric disorder: anxiety
(Volume 1), depression (Volume 2), or trauma (this volume). The series—
which may in the future include more titles—is based on my book *1001
Solution-Focused Questions: Handbook for Solution-Focused Interviewing* (Bannink, 2010a), originally written in Dutch and translated into English, German, and Korean.

I feel privileged that Insoo Kim Berg, co-founder of solution-focused
brief therapy (SFBT), wrote the Foreword of *1001 Solution-Focused Questions*
in 2006:

> SFBT is based on the respectful assumption that clients have
> the inner resources to construct highly individualized and uniquely
> effective solutions to their problems . . . The 1001 SF questions
> presented in this clear and well-written book will give the reader a
> very good idea of the importance of the precise use of language as a

---

1   The medical model uses the term *patient*; SFBT uses the term *client*.

tool in SFBT. Readers are invited to open themselves to a new light on interviewing clients.

The focus in each volume is on creating preferred futures and the pathways to get there. In addition to a description of the ways in which SFBT may be applied, each book contains exactly 101 SF questions that lie at the heart of SFBT. Over the years, I have collected more than 2,000 SF questions. It has been quite a challenge to select what I think are the best 101 questions for each volume. I admit I cheated a little by sometimes grouping multiple questions together and by changing some questions to the first person (n this volume, only questions therapists ask their clients are counted). As a result, you actually get far more than 101 questions! Questions for therapists themselves and questions clients may ask themselves (sometimes invited by their therapists) or may ask their therapists are also described, but are not included in the "101" list. At the end of each chapter, an overview of the SF questions is given. Some of the questions overlap with those in other chapters. Rather than repeating these questions, I have chosen to mention each SF question just once.

SFBT is a transdiagnostic approach. The reason I have nevertheless written separate volumes for different psychiatric disorders is to accommodate the many colleagues who are working with specific client groups. To give readers the opportunity to integrate the SF approach, this book introduces 40 exercises, 25 cases, and 18 stories.

This volume is aimed at all professionals working with trauma survivors, as well as their families and friends, who would prefer to adopt a (more) positive approach and/or would like to simply increase the range of techniques available to them. SF conversations with clients have proven to be more lighthearted than other kinds of conversations, ensuring less burnout for professionals.

Although the book is primarily aimed at professionals, I hope that people suffering from PTSD who don't see a therapist may also find useful information and helpful exercises within its pages.

It's about time to turn the tide on trauma treatment and shift the focus from reducing distress and merely *surviving* to building success and positively *thriving*.

—Fredrike Bannink
December 2014

1

Trauma

Introduction

*T*rauma (from the Greek word meaning "a wound") refers to either a physical injury or psychological shock or severe distress resulting from a traumatic experience. Psychological trauma is part of being human. Even so, most people don't develop posttraumatic stress disorder (PTSD). Epidemiological studies of the prevalence of PTSD in trauma-exposed populations show that resilience is the norm, not the exception. In this chapter, a short description of PTSD is given, followed by myths about trauma. My concept of *posttraumatic success* includes the 3 R's: *R*ecovery, en*R*ichment (posttraumatic growth), and *R*esilience. Understanding clients' resources helps therapists foster positive development as opposed to focusing on what is wrong with them, and to enable them to use what happened to them to make their lives *better instead of bitter.*

Posttraumatic Stress Disorder

Experiencing trauma is an essential part of being human; history is written in blood. Throughout evolution, people have been exposed to terrible events: accidents, medical complications or illnesses, childhood physical or sexual assaults or witnessing of such events, adult experiences of physical or sexual assault, warfare, policing and other occupations involving exposure to violence, or life- threatening natural disasters. To be distressed is a normal reaction to the horror, helplessness, and fear that are the critical elements of a traumatic experience.

The good news is that only a minority of people will develop PTSD, and with the passage of time symptoms will resolve in approximately two thirds of these (McFarlane & Yehuda, 1996). Data from the National Comorbidity Survey (NCS) show that although 50% to 60% of the U.S. population is exposed to traumatic experiences at some point, only 8% meet full criteria for PTSD (Kessler, Sonnega, Bromet, Higher, & Nelson, 1995).

Thus, most people who have gone through a traumatic experience will not develop PTSD. They may suffer acute symptoms like numbing, detachment, derealization, depersonalization or dissociation, nightmares, and thoughts and flashbacks of the event, and they may avoid stimuli that remind them of what happened. These symptoms may resolve themselves, usually within four weeks of the event.

Even though the symptoms of PTSD have been recognized throughout history, it wasn't until the 1980s that the diagnosis as we know it today came to be. Before that time, PTSD was referred to as *shell shock*, *combat fatigue*, or *war neurosis*.

The essential feature of PTSD is the development of characteristic symptoms following exposure to an extreme traumatic stressor involving direct personal experience of an event that involves actual or threatened death or serious injury or some other threat to one's physical integrity (like sexual violation); witnessing an event that involves death, injury, or a threat to the physical integrity of another person; learning about the unexpected or violent death, harm, or threat of death or injury experienced by a family member or other close person; or repeated exposure to distressing details of events, such as when police officers or therapists repeatedly hear details about sexual abuse.

Generally speaking, there is consensus on PTSD signs and symptoms, but there is an ongoing discussion about the definition of a *traumatic event*. Initially, a traumatic event was defined from the symptomatic perspective: If a person exhibited a specific set of (distress) symptoms, it was assumed that he or she had experienced a traumatic event. The underlying assumption was that traumatic events will cause signs of severe maladjustment in any individual and that the specific set of distress symptoms is similar in all those affected—that is, that they are universal. Later on, the focus shifted from distress symptoms to specifying the type of event, defined as being "outside the range of normal experience." The implicit assumption of a universal reaction to the event remained. Because this definition met with severe criticism, distress symptoms were added to the specification of the event: actual experience or threat of death or serious injury and a reaction to this involving fear, helplessness, and horror. The definition of a traumatic event in the fifth edition of the *Diagnostic and Statistical Manual of Mental Disorders* (DSM-5; American Psychiatric Association, 2013) no longer includes subjective distress reactions. The enduring difficulty in defining a traumatic event is reflected in the definitions in subsequent DSM classifications (De Jong, 2014).

However, no event can be universally traumatic. People report violent events as potentially traumatic only when these events are out of proportion to the setting in which they occurred, even if the events in other circumstances would not be classified as traumatizing (Horwitz & Wakefield, 2007; Spitzer & Wakefield, 2007). Therefore, in this book I will use the term *traumatic experience(s)* (of an event) instead of *traumatic event(s)*.

Complex PTSD (C-PTSD) is not a formal diagnosis, although many therapists use this concept. This type of PTSD is referred to as PTSD Dissociative Subtype in DSM-5, because complex trauma is often identified in conjunction with dissociative symptoms and/or personality disorders. Dissociative symptoms can be either experiences of feeling detached from one's own mind or body or experiences in which the world seems unreal, dreamlike, or distorted. Clients suffering from C-PTSD often have problems trusting other people, may have tendencies to harm themselves (i.e., via cutting or other self-injury, suicide attempts, and high-risk acting out, such as extreme drug or alcohol intoxication), and often have a borderline personality disorder, eating disorder, substance abuse or dependence, panic disorder, or schizoid or schizotypal personality disorder.

Roughly half of individuals with PTSD have comorbid major depressive disorder (Shalev et al., 1998) (see Volume 2: depression)

Myths about Trauma

One of the myths about stress and trauma is that there are only negative effects, including only negative *affect*. But research shows that positive and negative affect may exist concurrently during chronic stress, with positive affect having adaptive functions (Folkman & Moskowitz, 2000). However, many psychologists and psychiatrists became *pathologizers* and *victimologists* with a focus on assessing and curing individual suffering (to make miserable people less miserable). Therapists went about treating trauma within the disease–patient framework of repairing damage. This focus on pathology ("What's wrong with you?") generated several myths about stress and trauma:

- Everyone who has a traumatic experience will develop PTSD.
- People must have psychotherapy to get over PTSD.
- The only effective treatment for PTSD is long-term psychotherapy in which the client reexperiences or remembers everything that happened during the traumatic incident.
- There are only negative effects from trauma.

In the military, the police force, and other occupations where people are exposed to violence and disaster, detrimental ideas still exist, such as

"Seeking help will kill my career because I will be perceived in a negative light," "If I see a therapist, everyone will know about it," and "Therapy
doesn't work."

STORY 1. GIVE UP 13.6 YEARS OF YOUR LIFE

Doctor, Zoellner, and Feeny (2011) interviewed 184 persons seeking treatment for PTSD at two treatment sites in different regions
of the United States. They found that recollections of a traumatic
experience and avoidance of certain activities and thoughts, both
commonly conceived of as dysfunctional behaviors, had little cor-
relation to an individual's reported sense of well-being. However,
symptoms tied to heightened arousal, such as trouble sleeping,
irritability, and vigilance, were associated with lower quality of
life. Anxiety and depression were also associated with lower quality of life. The effect of avoidance on quality of life was limited
because it is a coping strategy and may, in the short term, improve
well-being.

The researchers found that, on average, a person suffering
from PTSD was willing to give up 13.6 years of his or her life to
live unburdened by the symptoms of the disorder. On average,
individuals were willing to accept a treatment with up to a 13%
chance of immediate death in order to achieve total relief of PTSD
symptoms.

Posttraumatic Success

My concept of *posttraumatic success* includes the 3 R's: *R*ecovery from PTSD symptoms, *R*esilience, and en*R*ichment (posttraumatic growth; Bannink, 2008a, 2014b). When therapists help clients to let their experiences make them better, there can be a range of outcomes. For some people, posttraumatic success implies a full or partial recovery from the symptoms of PTSD, and that is as far as they can go. For other people, posttraumatic success implies not only recovery from symptoms but also simultaneous posttraumatic growth. Often, posttraumatic growth and symptoms of PTSD coexist. For other people, posttraumatic success implies finding a resiliency that allows them to go on with their lives, often on their own, such that therapists will usually not see this group of trauma survivors in their office. The 3 R's are described below.

Recovery means a return or restoration from pathology to a normal, former condition. The term is derived from the medical model of treatment, where the relief of—or better still, the absence of—symptoms is the goal of treatment. Most treatments, such as cognitive behavioral therapy (CBT), EMDR (eye movement desensitization and reprocessing), and mindfulness-based therapy, are aimed at recovery, not at resilience or growth; they aim to relieve symptoms of PTSD by helping clients deal with traumatic experiences. In these treatments, clients explore their thoughts and feelings about the trauma; work through feelings of guilt, self-blame, and mistrust; and learn how to cope with and control intrusive memories and address problems in their lives and relationships.

Resilience refers to how people negotiate adversity to maintain their well-being. In recognizing and treating trauma aftereffects, our field often overlooks that the vast majority of people are resilient and come back from even the most horrific and intrusive traumas. Focusing on the negative aftereffects inadvertently helps people see themselves as damaged and unchangeable. Because early studies on trauma focused solely on the recovery of individuals seeking treatment, researchers have underestimated the potential for human *resilience*. Until recently, resilience was considered to be the exception, or worse: a pathological state in which individuals were not working through their problem. The usual response to high adversity is a relatively brief episode of depression and anxiety, followed by a return to the previous level of functioning.

Resilience is distinct from recovery. Bonanno (2004) states that the term *recovery* connotes a trajectory in which normal functioning temporarily gives way to (sub)threshold psychopathology, usually for a period of months or even years, and then gradually returns to pre-event levels. By contrast, resilience reflects the ability to maintain a stable equilibrium. A further distinction is that resilience is more than the simple absence of psychopathology. Recovering individuals often experience (sub)threshold symptom levels. Resilient individuals may experience transient perturbations in normal functioning (e.g., several weeks of sporadic preoccupation or restless sleep), but generally exhibit a stable trajectory of healthy functioning across time as well as the capacity for generative experiences and positive emotions. How to balance positive and negative emotions is described in Volume 1: Anxiety and Volume 2: Depression.

CASE 1. MY KIDS KEEP ME GOING

A therapist explained how she worked with soldiers. One of the things she did was to ask the soldiers what had helped them survive. The most common response was "My kids. They keep me going." Then the therapist typically proceeded to inquire how the kids were important and encouraged the soldiers to explain, as concretely as they could, how thinking about the children made the difference and enhanced their will to survive.

EnRichment or *posttraumatic growth* (PTG) means that people eventually arrive at a higher level of functioning than they had before the traumatic experience happened. This is a positive change, experienced as a result of the struggle with the traumatic experience(s) (Calhoun & Tedeschi, 2000). In other words, the experience is transformative and represents a *value-added* or *better-off-afterward* state. Other descriptions of this construct are *thriving* (O'Leary & Ickovics, 1995), *stress-related growth* (Park, Cohen, & Murch, 1996), *perceived benefits* (McMillen, Smith, & Fisher, 1997), and *adversarial growth* (Bohlmeijer & Bannink, 2013; Linley & Joseph, 2004).

If people are asked, "Did your difficult childhood make you stronger or weaker?" the reply is likely to be that it actually made them stronger. The following quote by Nietzsche has become famous: "What doesn't kill me makes me stronger." Five areas of growth may spring from adversity: (1) renewed appreciation for life, (2) enhanced personal strength, (3) identifying and acting on new possibilities for one's life, (4) improved interpersonal relationships, and (5) spiritual deepening. Data support this; 61% of imprisoned airmen tortured for years by the North Vietnamese said that they had benefited psychologically from their ordeal. What's more, the more severe their symptoms, the greater the posttraumatic growth (PTG).

PTG has been documented for many diverse areas of trauma and stress, including illness, bereavement, natural disasters, sexual assault, military combat, and terrorist attacks. It is a direct contrast to PTSD, where individuals find no benefit from trauma, only pain and anxiety (Haidt, 2006). Clients experiencing PTG say things like they have learned to appreciate what they have; they have experienced an increase in the depth of feeling good or bad, happy or sad, which they wouldn't want to be without; or they don't worry about silly things anymore. Sadly, it often takes a tragic event in our lives before we make these changes. Survivors and thrivers have much to teach those of us who haven't experienced such traumas about how to live.

STORY 2 A CREATIVE, POSITIVE FORCE

An example of PTG is Terry Waite, who, as an envoy for the Church of England, traveled to Lebanon to try to secure the release of four hostages. He himself was then held captive in solitary confinement from 1989 to 1991. Waite has commented, "Suffering is universal: You attempt to subvert it so that it does not have a destructive, negative effect. You turn it around so that it becomes a creative, positive force."

The relationship between recovery, resilience, and PTG is complex (Bannink, 2014b). Often PTSD symptoms occur simultaneously with PTG benefits. PTG may follow psychotherapy (see Chapter 3) or may occur during treatment. The focus on resilience and PTG should not come at the expense of empathy for the client's suffering. Tedeschi and Calhoun (2004) offer some caveats regarding PTG. They state that PTG occurs in the context of suffering and significant psychological struggle; it emerges from the struggle with coping, not from the trauma itself, which is not good in any way or desirable. Also, trauma is not necessary for growth. Finally, there are a significant number of people who experience little or no growth in their struggle with trauma, and this should be quite acceptable.

STORY 3. AN EXAMPLE OF POSTTRAUMATIC SUCCESS

Frankl (1963, p. 178) is often cited as an example of posttraumatic success (1963, p. 178): "What matters most of all is the attitude we take toward suffering" . He said of his stay in a German concentration camp that a prisoner who no longer believed in the future was doomed. Frankl described an incident where he staggered along in a row of prisoners on his way to the work area, in the cold and without food. At one point he found himself thinking about something else: He saw himself standing on the stage of an auditorium where he was giving a lecture about the psychology of the camp system. In this way he succeeded in lifting himself above the suffering of the moment and was able to view the torment as if it were already in the past. His focus on the future saved him for that moment. And his vision of the future became reality, as after the war he conducted many successful lecture tours. In his "logotherapy," Frankl explains that the meaning in suffering is resilience itself: The trick is to handle as well as possible the challenges that we face in life.

Dolan (1998) states that overcoming the immediate effects of abuse, loss, or other trauma and viewing oneself as a survivor rather than as a victim are helpful steps, but are ultimately not sufficient to help people fully regain the ability to live a life that is as compelling, joyous, and fulfilling as it used to be. People who remain at the survivor stage see life through the window of their survivorhood rather than enjoying the unobstructed vision of the world around them that they previously held. All experiences are evaluated in terms of how they resemble, differ from, mitigate, or compound the effects of past events. This diminishes the individual's ability to fully experience and enjoy life and is responsible for the flatness and depression reported by many people who categorize themselves as survivors. A third position may be added: that of a *thriver*. This signifies that the trauma doesn't define the person any longer and has just become one part of who he or she is.

The concept of *posttraumatic success* with children and their families is described in Bannink (2014b).

In the next chapter, we will take a closer look at solution-focused brief therapy and the many SF questions that lie at the heart of SFBT.

2

Solution-Focused Brief Therapy

Introduction

Solution-focused brief therapy helps clients develop a vision of a better future and steps they may take to make that happen. In this chapter, a description of SFBT is followed by a short description of its theory, history, indications, and its research.

SF questions lie at the heart of SFBT: They invite clients to think differently, to notice positive differences, and to help make desired changes in their lives. Four basic SF questions are presented in this chapter.

Solution-Focused Brief Therapy

SFBT is the pragmatic application of a set of principles and tools, probably best described as finding the direct route to what works. *If something is working (better), do more of it; if something isn't working, do something else*. The nature of SFBT is nonacademic; the pursuit is finding what works for this client at this moment in this context. The emphasis is on constructing solutions as a counterweight to the traditional emphasis on the analysis of problems. SFBT does not claim to solve people's problems or to cure their disorders. However, it claims to help clients achieve their preferred future, so classification or diagnosis of problems is often irrelevant. Of course, when clients achieve their preferred future, their problem might . . . or might not . . . have gone away (Bannink & Jackson, 2011).

The aim of SFBT is to assist clients in developing a mental picture of a more satisfying future, and to direct both clients and therapists toward a deeper awareness of the strengths and resources that clients can use in turning vision into reality (De Jong & Berg, 2002). SFBT is a competence-based approach that minimizes emphasis on past failings and problems and instead focuses on clients' strengths, previous successes, and exceptions (times when the problem could have happened but didn't). In solutions-building, clients are seen as experts with regard to their own lives.

SF therapists always listen for openings in conversations that are often problem-saturated. These openings can be about what clients would like to be different in their lives, exceptions, competencies and resources, and who or what might be helpful in taking next steps.

Clients' solutions are not necessarily related to any identified problem. They are encouraged to find out what works and increase the frequency of these useful behaviors. Improvement is often realized by redirecting attention from dissatisfaction about a status quo to a positive goal and beginning to take steps in that direction. This process of shifting attention uses three steps:

1. Acknowledge the problem ("This must be hard for you").
2. Suggest a desire for change ("So I guess you would like things to be different . . .").
3. Ask about the preferred future ("How would you like things to be different?").

SFBT is based on *social constructionism*. This theory claims that the individual's notion of what is real—including his or her sense of the nature of problems, abilities, and possible solutions—is constructed in daily life in communication with others. People confer meaning on events in communication with others, and in this process language plays a central role. Shifts in perceptions and definitions occur within frames of reference in society; conferring meaning is not an isolated activity. Individuals adjust the way in which they confer meaning under the influence of the society in which they live.

The social constructionist perspective can be used to examine how therapists and conversations with them may contribute to the creation of a new reality for clients. Clients' capacity for change is related to their ability to begin to see things differently. These shifts in the perception and definition of reality occur in the SF conversation about the preferred future and exceptions. SF questions map out clients' goals and solutions, which are assumed to be present in their life already.

De Shazer, Berg, and their colleagues developed SFBT during the 1980s. They expanded upon the findings of Watzlawick, Weakland, and Fisch (1974), who found that the attempted solution often perpetuates the problem and that an understanding of the origins of the problem is not (always) necessary. De Shazer's (1985) propositions include the following:

- The development of a solution is not necessarily related to the problem. An analysis of the problem isn't useful in finding solutions, whereas an analysis of exceptions to the problem is.
- Clients are the experts. They determine the goal and the road to achieving it.
- If it is not broken, don't fix it. Leave alone what is positive in the perception of clients.
- If something works, continue with it, even though it may be something different from what was expected.
- If something doesn't work, do something else. More of the same leads nowhere.

They discovered that three types of therapist behavior made clients four times as likely to talk about solutions, change, and resources:

1. Asking *eliciting questions*: "What would you like to see instead of the problem?"
2. Asking *questions about details*: "What exactly did you do differently?"

3. Giving *verbal rewards* by giving compliments and asking *competence questions*: "How did you manage to come here today?"

SFBT is *indicated* for virtually all work environments as a monotherapy or in combination with a problem-focused therapy. Depending on the nature of the problem, a problem-focused approach (e.g., pharmacotherapy) may be chosen, in which the supplementary use of SFBT is often valuable. The attitude of the therapist, attention to goal formulation, and tapping into the often surprisingly large arsenal of competencies possessed by clients and their environment are key elements in a successful outcome. SFBT is also suitable for treating addiction-related problems due to the considerable attention paid to clients' motivation to change their behavior.

Can SFBT also be applied in cases of chronic and severe mental illness? The answer is that in these cases also, there are always people who can, as much as possible, beyond and outside their chronic and/or severe mental illness, reclaim their life and identity. O'Hanlon and Rowan (2003, p. ix) state,

> Over time, we have become increasingly convinced that traditional pathological language, labels, belief systems, and treatment methods can inhibit positive change. In fact, a hopeless situation can be engendered with unintentional and unfortunate cues from treatment milieus, therapists, family members, and oneself. Iatrogenic discouragement—that which is inadvertently induced by treatment—is often the result of such an unfortunate view of human perception and behavior.

Biological treatments seem to be strictly problem-focused. Nevertheless, it makes a difference if clients have the idea that "the depression will disappear" or that they (in positive terms) will become "energetic, active, or relaxed." An SF approach to *pharmacological treatment* may consist of encouraging clients to give a detailed description of what the first signs of recovery might look like, assuming that the medication takes effect, and of how the recovery will further manifest itself. Clients are asked what they themselves can add to the effect of the medication, or what they can do to create an environment in which the medication will have the maximum effect in helping them to pull through.

STORY 3. SHOT BY A POISONED ARROW

If a man is shot by a poisoned arrow and says, "Don't take this arrow away before you find out exactly by whom and from where and how it was shot," the man's death is inevitable.

—BUDDHA

SFBT requires no extensive *diagnosis*. "Interventions can initiate change without the therapist's first understanding, in any detail, what has been going on" (De Shazer, 1985, p. 119). One may choose to commence treatment immediately and if necessary pay attention to diagnostics at a later stage. Severe psychiatric disorders or a suspicion thereof justifies the decision to conduct a thorough diagnosis, since the tracing of the underlying organic pathology, for instance, has direct therapeutic consequences.

During the first or follow-up sessions, it will automatically become clear whether an advanced diagnosis is necessary—for example, if there is a visible deterioration in the client's condition or if the treatment fails to give positive results. One could think of *stepped diagnosis* as being analogous to *stepped care* (Bakker, Bannink, & Macdonald, 2010). Duncan (2010) also states that, unlike with medical treatments, diagnosis is an ill-advised starting point for psychotherapy. Diagnosis in mental health is not correlated with outcome or length of stay, and giving the *dodo verdict* (all psychotherapies are equal and have won prizes) cannot provide reliable guidance regarding the best approach to solving a problem. Furthermore, a diagnosis should not be a label but should lead to the kind of support that allows clients to reach their full potential.

Is it possible to solve problems without even talking about them? The answer is yes. Just say, "Suppose there is a solution," and then invite clients to ask themselves the following questions:

- "What difference will this solution make in my life and those of others who are important to me?"
- "What will I be doing (and/or thinking and feeling) differently?"
- "Who will be the first to notice?"
- "What will be the first small sign that a solution is under way?"
- "Who will be the least surprised?"
- "What else will be better?"

EXERCISE 1. IT'S NOT NECESSARY
TO KNOW THE PROBLEM

Do this exercise with a colleague to find out that it is not necessary to know the problem in order to examine the goal and solutions. The other person says, "I feel too embarrassed to talk about my problem, but I need help now, because I can't go on like this any longer!" You respond, "Supposing there were a solution, what difference would that make for you?" (or "How will you know?" or "How will that help you?"). Or ask some of the questions listed before this exercise.

SFBT often proves useful in *crisis intervention*. The available time does not lend itself to an elaborate diagnosis, and clients in crisis benefit from regaining confidence in their personal competencies and from a future-oriented approach. Think of questions such as "How do you manage to carry on?" or "What has helped you in the past weeks, even if only slightly?" Commonly, clients relinquish competence to the therapist ("You tell me what I should do")—a pitfall that can be avoided with SFBT.

Nowadays, the SF approach is being successfully applied to psychotherapy, coaching, conflict management, leadership, education, and sports. Useful books describing the SF approach with trauma survivors have been written by Bannink (2014b), Dolan (1991, 1998), Furman (1998), Henden (2011), and O'Hanlon and Bertolino (1998).

SFBT is based on over 20 years of theoretical development, clinical practice, and empirical *research*. Franklin, Trepper, Gingerich, and McCollum (2012) state that SFBT is an evidence-based form of psychotherapy. For information on the evidence-based practice of SFBT, see also Macdonald (2011). Meta-analytic reviews of the outcome research show SFBT to have a small to moderate positive outcome for a broad range of topics and populations. When SFBT has been compared with established treatments in recent, well-designed studies, it has been shown to be equivalent to other evidence-based approaches, producing results in substantially less time and at less cost. Gingerich and Peterson (2013) reviewed 43 studies. Thirty-two (74%) of the studies reported significant positive benefit from SFBT; 10 (23%) reported positive trends. The strongest evidence of effectiveness came in the treatment of depression in adults, where four separate studies found SFBT to be comparable to well-established alternative treatments. Three studies examined length of treatment, and all found that SFBT used fewer sessions than other forms of psychotherapies. These studies provide evidence that SFBT is an effective treatment for a wide variety of behavioral and psychological outcomes and, in addition, is briefer and therefore less costly than traditional approaches.

Problem-Talk or Solutions-Talk

SF therapists use *operant conditioning* principles during the sessions. Operant conditioning deals with reinforcement and punishment to change behavior. SF therapists use, whenever possible, positive reinforcement of *solutions-talk* (conversations about goals, exceptions, possibilities, competencies, and resources) and negative punishment (nonreinforcement) of *problem-talk* (conversations about problems, causes, impossibilities, and weaknesses). This doesn't mean that clients are not allowed to talk about problems or that SFBT is problem-phobic. Therapists listen respectfully to their clients' stories, but they don't seek any details about the presented problems, thus not reinforcing problem-talk (see Table 2.1).

TABLE 2.1

The Differences between Problem-Talk and Solutions-Talk

Problem-Talk	Solutions-Talk
Conversations about clients' problems, what they don't want, causes, negative emotions, disadvantages, deficits, risks, failures, and the undesired/feared future	Conversations about what clients want, exceptions, positive emotions, advantages, strengths and resources, opportunities, successes, and the preferred future

EXERCISE 2. RAISE YOUR
PERCENTAGE OF SOLUTIONS-TALK

What percentage of time in your intakes and/or treatment do you spend asking clients about their preferred future, strengths, successes, and what works in their life? Ten percent? Twenty percent? Fifty percent or maybe 0%? Supposing you were the client, how would you like your therapist to spend his or her time during your therapy? Would you like to be invited to talk about your strengths, successes, and solutions? You probably would! So why not raise the percentage of time by just 10 percent (i.e., if you use 10%, make it 20%) and notice what difference this makes both for your clients and for yourself.

Solution-Focused Questions

The answers you get depend on the questions you ask. *Solution-focused questions* form a large part of the SF therapist's tool kit; they lie at the heart of SFBT. These questions invite clients to think about transformation and help them make desired changes in their life. Asking SF questions is not meant to gather information so as to render the therapist an expert on clients' lives. Rather, these questions are an invitation to think differently, to notice positive differences, and to help clients make progress when they are stuck.

The attitude of SF therapists is one of *not knowing*. They allow themselves to be informed by their clients and the context of their clients' lives, which determines in what way solutions are devised. Another aspect of this attitude is *leading from one step behind*. Therapists, metaphorically speaking, stand behind their clients and tap them on the shoulder with SF questions, inviting them to look at their preferred future and, in order to achieve this, to envision a wide horizon of possibilities.

With SF questions, therapists ask clients to describe the smallest signs of progress and encourage them to carry on with the smallest and easiest of these. This enables clients to experience in a safe and gradual manner control over the problem, without becoming afraid or feeling overwhelmed by tasks that they are not yet ready for. These small changes pave the way for increasingly larger changes. SF questions are effective in encouraging clients to participate in and develop their own treatment plan, within which, implicitly, a context of hope is created (Dolan, 1991).

EXERCISE 3. MORE HELPFUL QUESTIONS

Consider a typical problematic situation. Write down the typical questions you ask yourself about it. Examine these questions closely. Does asking them help you feel better or worse? Does asking them help move you forward to where you want to be or merely give you an explanation for why you are stuck or can't change? If your questions are not helping you, find more helpful questions.

SF questions are different from closed ones; they tend to narrow clients' focus, while *open questions* tend to widen their perceptual field. Open questions are more likely to focus on the client's frame of reference. An example of a closed question would be "Did you manage?" An example of an open question would be "How did you manage?" Open questions invite clients to reflect as much as possible and to provide answers that go beyond a mere yes or no. *How, what, who, where,* and *when* questions are all examples of open questions. *Why* questions are not part of SFBT, because they tend to elicit analyses of possible underlying causes of the problem and may be experienced as judgmental or confrontational.

Microanalysis of dialogue (Bavelas, Coates, & Johnson, 2000) aims for a detailed and replicable examination of observable communication sequences between therapists and clients. Two tools are being used during analysis of video recordings of the dialogues: *analysis of formulations* and *analysis of questions*, in which *how questions function* (intentionally or not) as therapeutic interventions is analyzed (see Volume 1: Anxiety). Microanalysis can complement outcome research by providing evidence about what therapists do in their sessions and how the co-constructive nature of *language* is important in dialogues.

Co-constructing a dialogue may be compared to a dance or a duet between therapists and clients. SF ideas for *paying attention to language* include the following:

- Change "if" to "when": "If I get over this trauma, I will be able to do what I want" becomes "When I get over this trauma, I will be able to do what I want."

- Change "can't" to "not yet": "I can't put the past behind me" becomes "I haven't yet been able to put the past behind me."

- Move problems from internal to external: "I am depressed" becomes "Depression has been visiting me for a while"; "I am a negative person" becomes "Negativity speaks to me regularly, and mostly I listen to what it says."

- Use the past tense when talking about problems and the future tense when talking about what clients want different in their lives: "I will never get over what happened to me" becomes "So until now I haven't been able to get over what happened to me. How will my life be different when I am able to do that?"

EXERCISE 4. OPENING QUESTION

What *opening question* do you start the first session with? Do you opt for a problem-focused question ("What is the problem?" or "What is bothering you?")? Do you choose a neutral question ("What brings you here?")? Do you ask a question that implies that you will work hard ("What can I do for you?")? Or do you ask an SF question ("What would you like to be different in your life?" or "What would you like to see instead of the problem?" or "When can we stop seeing each other?")? Try out all possibilities and notice the differences in clients' reactions and differences in the mood of the sessions.

Four Basic SF Questions

Four basic SF questions (Bannink, 2007, 2010a) can be used at the start of therapy or at the beginning of each session (e.g., "What are your best hopes for this session?"):

1. "What are your best hopes?"
2. "What difference will that make?"
3. "What works?"
4. "What will be the next signs of progress?" or "What will be your next step?"

The *first basic SF question* is: "What are your best hopes?"

Hope is one of the most powerful attitudes, emotions, thoughts, beliefs, and motivators. It is vital to human beings; it keeps people alive. It gets people out of bed in the morning. Hope keeps us going, even in the face of severe adversity. Hope whispers "Try it one more time" when the world says "Give up."

Offering a vision that change is possible and that there are better ways to deal with the situation is important in therapy. SFBT fits well with this value, because solutions-building is about the development of a well-defined goal through asking about clients' best hopes and what differences those will make. These questions encourage clients to develop a detailed vision of what their lives might look like. It fosters hope and motivation and promotes self-determination. SFBT counters any tendency to raise false hope in clients; they define their own visions for change and, as experts about their situation, clarify what parts of their preferred future can and cannot happen.

Questions about hope are different from questions about expectations. "What do you expect from therapy?" invites clients to look at the therapist for the solution to the problem.

The *second basic SF question* is: "What difference will that make?" Clients are invited to describe their preferred future in positive, concrete, and realistic terms. How will they react, and how will they interact differently? How will their life be different? What will they be doing differently so others will know that they have reached their preferred future? Often clients describe the preferred future without the problem that brought them to therapy, although some clients describe their preferred future with the problem still present, but without it bothering them so much anymore.

De Shazer (1991) states that difference itself is an important tool for therapists and clients. In and of themselves, differences don't work spontaneously. Only when recognized can they be put to work to make a difference. "What difference will it make when your best hopes are met?" "How will your life be different?" "What will you be doing differently?" "How will your relationship with the other person(s) differ?"

Finding exceptions is another way of asking about differences. "When the problem is/was there to a lesser extent, what is/was different? What are/were you doing differently? What are/were others doing differently?" or "When is/was there a glimpse of the preferred future already?" This reveals what was working in better times, and things that were helpful in the past may be used anew. Also, *scaling questions* help to find positive differences. Scaling questions can be asked about progress, hope, motivation, and confidence (see Chapter 6).

EXERCISE 5. SUPPOSE THINGS COULD CHANGE

Invite clients to think of something they would like to see changed. Ask, "Supposing things could change, what difference would that make?" "What else would be different?" "What else?" See how clients will probably come up with more things than you or they imagined they would (this is called the *upward arrow technique* as a counterweight to the downward arrow technique used in CBT, described in Bannink [2012a, 2014]).

CASE 2. WHAT DIFFERENCE WILL IT MAKE?

The client, a survivor of sexual abuse, says she might feel happier if she were able to sleep better, without having nightmares. The therapist asks, "What difference will it make when you sleep better?" The woman replies that she might feel more fit and that she would cautiously begin to believe that better sleep without disturbances is possible. The therapist then asks her what difference that slightly better feeling and bit of hope will make in her life. She answers that

she would go outside more and would probably be nicer to her children and husband. With these questions, the client's vision of her
preferred future is further magnified, which increases her hope for
a better life.

The third basic SF question is: "What works?" Therapists may start by
inquiring about *pretreatment change* (see Chapter 4). Most clients have tried
other ideas before seeing a therapist. It is a common assumption that clients
begin to change when therapists start to help them with the problem, but
change is happening in all clients' lives. When asked, two thirds of clients
in psychotherapy report positive change between the time they made the
appointment and the first session (Weiner-Davis, de Shazer, & Gingerich,
1987). Exploration of pretreatment change often reveals new and useful
information. When clients report that things are better, even just a little bit,
therapists ask competence questions: "How did you do that?" "How did you
decide to do that?" "Where did you get this good idea?"

Exception-finding questions are frequently used to find out what works
(see Chapter 6). Those questions are new to many clients (and therapists),
who are more accustomed to problem-focused questions. When asked
about exceptions, which are the keys to solutions, they may start noticing
them for the first time. Solutions are often built from formerly unrecognized positive differences. Therapists, having explored these exceptions,
then compliment clients for all the things they have done.

A *scaling question* may be added: "On a scale where 10 equals you reached your preferred future and 0 equals the moment you picked up the phone to make this appointment, where would you say you are right now?" (see Chapter 6).

The *fourth basic SF question* is: "What will be the next signs of progress?" or "What will be your next step?" By asking "What will be *your* next step?" therapists invites clients to—maybe for the first time—actually think about what they themselves can do to ameliorate the situation instead of waiting for other(s) or the therapist to provide a solution.

This question is only asked when clients want or need to go up further on the scale of progress. When the current state is the best possible state at the moment, then the conversation continues by asking clients how they can maintain the status quo. The question about the next signs of progress is open as to who should do what and when. A sign of progress may also be something that could happen without the clients taking action. Instead of focusing on the inner life of clients and why the problems arose, SFBT invites clients to move into action.

The four basic SF questions can be seen as *skeleton keys*: keys that fit in many different locks. You don't have to explore and analyze each lock (e.g., analyze each problem) before you can use these keys. The keys can be used for all Axis I and Axis II disorders, including PTSD.

Grant and O'Connor (2010) explored the differential effects of problem-focused and solution-focused questions in a coaching context. They found that problem-focused questions (e.g., questions like "What is your problem?" or "What is bothering you?") reduce negative affect and increase self-efficacy, but don't increase the understanding of the nature of the problem or enhance positive affect. SF questions increase positive affect, decrease negative affect, and increase self-efficacy as well as *insight and understanding* of the nature of the problem.

CASE 3. WORKING FROM THE FUTURE BACK

SFBT works from the future back. The client with several symptoms of PTSD is invited to think about the following questions:

- "Suppose I made a full recovery. What would have helped me recover from what I've experienced?"
- "How would I have found the courage to do that?"
- "What would have given me the strengths to make these changes?"
- "How would important people in my life (partner, friends, colleagues) tell that I had made a full recovery?"
- "What, in their opinion, helped me to recover?"

STORY 5. THE SHATTERED VASE

The metaphor of the shattered vase is often used in working with trauma survivors. Posttraumatic growth involves the rebuilding of the shattered assumptive world. Imagine that one day you accidentally knock a treasured vase off its perch. It smashes into tiny pieces. What do you do? Do you try to put the vase back together as it was? Do you collect the pieces and drop them in the rubbish, as the vase is a total loss? Or do you pick up the beautiful colored pieces and use them to make something new—such as a colorful mosaic? When adversity strikes, people often feel that at least some part of them—be it their views of the world, sense of themselves, relationships—has been smashed. Those who try to put their lives back together exactly as they were remain fractured and vulnerable. But those who accept the breakage and build themselves anew become more resilient and open to new ways of living.

These changes do not necessarily mean that people will be free of the memories of what has happened to them, the grief they experience, or other forms of distress. It means that their lives become more meaningful in light of what happened.

SF questions in this chapter are:

1. "How would you like things to be different?"
2. "What exactly did you do differently?"
3. "Suppose there is a solution. What difference will that make in your life and in the lives of important others? What will you be doing (and/or

thinking and feeling) differently? Who will be the first to notice? What will be the first small sign that a solution is under way? Who will be the least surprised? What else will be better?"

4. "What has helped you in the past weeks, even if only slightly?"

5. "When can we stop seeing each other?"

6. "What are your best hopes? What difference will that make?

7. "What works?"

8. "What will be the next signs of progress?" or "What will be your next step?"

9. "What difference will it make when your best hopes are fulfilled? How will your life be different? What will you be doing differently? How will your relationship with other person(s) differ? How will they react differently?"

10. "When the problem is/was there to a lesser extent, what is/was different then? What are/were you doing differently? What are/were other people doing differently?"

11. "When is/was there a glimpse of your preferred future already (the goal)?"

12. "Supposing things could change, what difference will that make? What else will be different? What else?"

13. "How did you do that? How did you decide to do that? Where did you get this good idea?"

14. "On a scale where 10 equals you have reached your preferred future and 0 equals the moment you picked up the phone to make this appoint-

ment, where would you say you are right now?" (and follow-up scaling questions).

In the next chapter, we will look at several traditional therapeutic approaches to trauma as well as the SF approach. An overview of the differences between these approaches will be given. Traditional and SF approaches may be combined in helping clients survive and thrive.

3

Therapeutic Approaches to Trauma

Introduction

In this chapter, several problem-focused approaches to trauma as well as the SF approach are briefly described. Slowly but surely, a shift from a deficit focus to a resource focus has become noticeable in psychology and psychiatry. In this chapter, an overview of the differences between the two paradigms is given. Traditional and SF approaches may also be combined in helping clients survive and thrive.

Traditional Approaches to Trauma

Most psychotherapeutic models still apply the pathology model. Their aim is to reduce distress by using the problem-solving paradigm. Among these models are psychoanalytic, client-centered, and cognitive behavioral therapy (CBT) approaches. Lately there has been a noticeable shift in focus in

CBT. For example, Beck (2011) also emphasizes the positive in CBT. She states that most clients, especially those with depression, tend to focus unduly on the negative. Their difficulty in processing positive data leads them to develop a distorted sense of reality. To counteract this feature of depression, therapists should help clients to attend to the positive. According to Beck, clients are invited to:

- Elicit their strengths ("What are some of my strengths and positive qualities?") at the evaluation of therapy (FB: In my opinion, this is a bit late)
- Find positive data from the preceding week ("What positive things have happened since I was here last?")
- Seek data contrary to their negative automatic thoughts and beliefs ("What is the positive evidence that perhaps my thought isn't true?")
- Look for positive data ("What does this say about me?)
- Note instances of their positive coping

Furthermore, the therapeutic alliance should be used to demonstrate that therapists see clients as valuable human beings. Therapists can suggest homework to facilitate their clients' experiencing of pleasure and achievement.

Bannink (2012a, 2014a) developed a new form of CBT that she calls *Positive CBT*. In this approach, SFBT, positive psychology, and traditional CBT are integrated. For example, in positive CBT, functional behavior analyses are made of exceptions to the problem instead of the problem itself.

Monitoring is about exceptions, and the downward arrow technique, which focuses on beliefs that underpin negative reactions to a given situation, is replaced with the upward arrow technique, which focuses on beliefs that underpin positive reactions and exceptions to the problem.

The goal of *eye movement desensitization and reprocessing* (EMDR; Shapiro, 2001) is to process traumatic memories, reducing their influence and allowing clients to develop more adaptive coping mechanisms. EMDR uses a structured eight-phase approach to address the past, present, and future aspects of a traumatic memory that has been dysfunctionally stored.

Imagery rescripting (ImRs) modifies a distressing image to change associated negative thoughts, feelings, and/or behaviors. Arntz and Weertman (1999) describe the use of ImRs to treat nightmares, posttraumatic stress disorder, bereavement, intrusive images, and eating disorders. ImRs is used not only to overcome problems, but also to help clients to develop a positive view of themselves and to promote self-determination and well-being.

Imagery can be either positive or negative. From a problem-focused perspective, negative imagery can be removed or transformed, whereas from an SF perspective, positive imagery can be created or enhanced. For example, Vasquez and Buehler (2007) found that imagining future success enhances people's motivation to achieve it. A positive image of oneself in the future motivates action by helping people to articulate their goals clearly and develop behaviors that will allow them to fulfill those goals. Thus, the very act of imagining future events not only makes those events seem more likely, but also helps to bring them about.

Mindfulness-based cognitive therapy (MBCT) combines meditation rooted in Buddhist thought and Western CBT. It helps increase a wide, open awareness as well as focused attention and reduces automatic responding. Mindfulness involves paying attention to changing moment-to-moment experience, whether it be pleasant, unpleasant, or neutral.

Compassion-focused therapy (CFT) aims to develop care and affiliative-focused motivation, attention, emotion, behavior, and thinking. Skills include the use of imagery, building the compassionate self, and using the sense of a compassionate self to engage with areas of personal difficulty. As an example of compassionate rescripting, clients who are trained in the compassionate self approach a difficult memory, holding the compassionate position as they watch the scene unfolding. Then gradually, with the compassionate self, they might bring new things into the scene (e.g., helpers) and begin to decide on new endings (Brewin et al., 2009; Gilbert, 2010).

Acceptance and commitment therapy (ACT) teaches clients to notice, accept, and embrace traumatic experiences (Hayes, Strosahl, & Wilson (2003). The premise of ACT is that psychological suffering is usually caused by experiential avoidance, cognitive entanglement, and resulting psychological rigidity that leads to a failure to take needed steps in accord with core values.

Positive psychology (PP) is an academic discipline principally concerned with understanding positive human thought, feeling, and behavior; an empirical pursuit of systematically understanding psychological phenomena; and finally an applied discipline in which interventions are created and employed. PP consists of a family of constructs such as optimism, hope, self-efficacy, self-esteem, positive emotions, flow, happiness, and gratitude.

PP is the study of what makes life worth living and what enables individuals and communities to thrive. It is the study of the conditions and processes that lead to optimal functioning in individuals, relationships, and work (Bannink, 2009a, 2012b). PP represents those efforts of professionals to help people optimize human functioning by acknowledging strengths as well as deficiencies, and environmental resources in addition to stressors. The study of mental health is distinct from and complementary to the long-standing interest in mental illness, its prevalence, and its remedies (Keyes & Lopez, 2005). Bannink and Jackson (2011) describe a comparison between PP and SFBT.

The SF Approach to Trauma

Medical diseases are commonly characterized by a deficit, and treatments are designed to target—directly or indirectly—that deficit, so that the patient is cured or at least not hindered by the deficit anymore. The history of psychiatry has been dominated by a similar deficit focus. Treatments have been developed to remove or ameliorate the presumed deficit, even if assumptions on the specific nature of the deficits may often have been speculative. Such a deficit focus applies to models of pharmacological treatments as well as psychotherapeutic ones, such as psychoanalysis or CBT, that aim to solve an underlying conflict or to change maladaptive thinking and behaviors. This focus on deficits has a number of limitations: For example, it may strengthen clients' negative image and reduce their sense of control, leaving them passive recipients of expert care. More important is that the deficit focus in psychiatric research has produced, at best, limited progress in developing more effective treatments since the 1980s (Priebe, Omer, Giacco, & Slade, 2014).

Not all therapeutic models, however, have been developed to target deficits. Instead, a number of models aim to tap into the strengths of clients and utilize their positive personal and social resources. Furthermore, data from 40 years of outcome research in psychotherapy provide strong empirical evidence for privileging the client's role in the change process (Miller et al., 1997. Clients, not therapists, make therapy work. As a result, therapy should be organized around their resources, perceptions, experiences, and ideas. The most potent factor of a successful outcome, clients and their propensities for change, is left out of the medical model in traditional psychotherapy.

The problem-solving model in psychotherapy assumes a necessary connection between a problem and its solution, as in modern medicine. This assumption underlies the field's emphasis on assessing problems before making interventions. However, De Shazer (1985) and Bakker, Bannink, and Macdonald (2010) state that it is not necessary to start treatment with the assessment of problems. As mentioned earlier, the aim of SFBT is to assist clients in describing a detailed vision of their preferred future, and to direct both clients and therapists toward a deeper awareness of the strengths and resources that clients can use in turning vision into reality. O'Hanlon (1999) offers SF guidelines for working with trauma. First, therapists should find out what clients are seeking to gain from therapy and how they will know when therapy has been successful. Therapists should ascertain that clients are safe: safe from suicide, homicide, and other potentially dangerous situations. Another guideline is that therapists don't need to assume that clients should always work through traumatic memories; from an SF viewpoint, every case is different. Therapists should look for strengths and resources; their focus should be on underlining how clients made it through the traumatic experiences and what they have done to cope, survive, and maybe thrive since then. They should look for nurturing and healthy relationships and role models clients had or have. Current skills in other areas should also be looked for. Clients should have the opportunity to tell therapists how they stopped themselves from acting on destructive impulses and were able to seek therapy, despite enduring the aftereffects of trauma. Each part of the clients' experience should be validated and supported. Therapists should not give the impression that clients' futures are determined by trauma. Self-blaming or invalidating identity stories clients have or have accepted from others should also be challenged and rewritten (see Chapter 7).

In this model, *exposure therapy* may be a valuable addition (e.g., when clients think exposure therapy will help them move forward, as suggested by their therapists, or if they choose themselves to confront difficult situations), but is not a sine qua non.

EXERCISE 6. THREE QUESTIONS TO BUILD HAPPINESS

The following three questions invite clients to build happiness (Isebaert, 2007). Even though it may be difficult for clients to find out what they feel good about, given the negative events they have been going through, they may benefit by repeating this exercise at the end of every day for some weeks or even months.

1. "What did I do today that I feel good about?"

2. "What has someone else done that I'm happy with? Did I react in such a way that this person will perhaps do something like that again?"

3. "What else do I see, hear, feel, smell, or taste that I like?"

SF questions inviting clients to think about *their coping during the traumatic experience* include the following:

- "How was I able to cope with what happened?"
- "How was I able to keep at least some control over the situation?"
- "What did I do to master my emotions?"
- "Which small aspect of the situation was I able to influence?"
- "What did I do well during the event?"
- "What did I do to prevent the situation from becoming even worse?"
- "Can I still discover something human in the person(s) who did this to me?"

- "Supposing there were one thing I did during the event that I were pleased about, what would it be?"

CASE 4. AT LEAST SOME INFLUENCE

A friend was forced to stop his car by four men, and they told him to sit in the back. While they were driving around, they threatened to kill him. Instead of panicking, he was able to think of a plan: He asked the guys what their personal strengths were. After a good laugh, the men indeed started to talk about their strengths. They eventually allowed him to leave the car and drove off. Whether the man's plan saved his life, we will never know, but at least he was able to influence some aspects of the situation.

SF questions to ask clients regarding *their coping after the traumatic experience* include the following:

- "How have you managed to survive?"
- "What helps you deal with what you've experienced?"
- "What else have you been through that was difficult, and what helped you then?"
- "Which of the things that helped you then could be useful to you again now?"

- "Do you know anyone else who has been through the same ordeal? What has helped that person deal with it?"
- "What does it mean for you to have survived these events?" or "What was good about this experience?"
- "If a miracle were to happen in the middle of the night and you overcame the consequences of these events well enough that you didn't have to come here anymore and you were (relatively) satisfied with your life, what would be different then?" or "Suppose you wake up tomorrow and your past is no longer messing with your future. What is the first sign you'll notice?"
- "What will you be doing differently when these traumatic memories are less of a problem in your daily life?"
- "What difference will those healing changes make in your life when they have lasted for a longer period of time (days, weeks, months, years)? What difference will they make in your relationships with important people in your life?"
- "What difference will the changes you've accomplished make for future generations of your family?"
- "What will be the smallest sign that things are going better? What difference will that make for you? What will be the next smallest sign? And the one after that?"
- "How will you be able to tell that you're handling things a little better or that this is a little easier for you?"
- "How could you regain hope that life can get easier in the future?"

- "What did the event(s) *not* change, and how did you manage that?"
- "What things in your life do you wish to maintain despite what has happened?"
- "What helps you keep traumatic images (intrusions) and memories under control?"
- "On a scale of 10 to 0, where 10 equals you are handling what's happened very well and 0 equals you cannot handle what's happened at all, where are you now?" (and follow-up scaling questions).
- "How do you now manage to sometimes feel safe and have control of your life?"
- "How can you comfort yourself? How do you do that?"
- "Who can comfort you now, even if only a little bit?"
- "How do you manage to come out of the dissociation?" or "How do you manage to stop hurting yourself? How do you do that? What else helps in this respect?"
- "How will you celebrate your victory over what happened to you?"

Differences in Approaches to Trauma

Table 3.1 shows a comparison between traditional approaches to trauma and the SF approach. It explains how the paradigm shift from the problem-solving to the solutions-building approach is applied in helping clients survive and thrive.

TABLE 3.1

Differences in Therapeutic Approaches to Trauma

Traditional Approaches to Trauma	The SF Approach to Trauma
Past- and problem-focused	Future- and solution-focused
Diagnosis before treatment	Stepped diagnosis
Focus on negative emotions	Focus on positive emotions with acknowledgment of negative ones
Term *patient* (medical model)	Term *client* (nonmedical model)
Therapist's theory of change	Client's theory of change
Conversations about what patient doesn't want (the problem)	Conversations about what client wants to have instead of the problem
Avoidance goals	Approach goals
Deficit model: Patient is viewed as damaged. How is the patient affected by the traumatic experience(s)?	Resource model: Client is viewed as influenced but not damaged, having strengths and resources. How did the client respond to traumatic experience(s)?
Looking for weaknesses and problems	Looking for strengths and solutions: success analysis
Patients are (sometimes) seen as not motivated (resistance)	Clients are seen as always motivated, but their goal may differ from that of the therapist

Remembering and expressing negative affect are goals of treatment	Goals are individualized for each client; increasing positive affect may be the goal of treatment
Therapist confronts	Therapist accepts the client's view and asks, "How is that helpful?"
Conversations about impossibilities	Acknowledgment, validation, and conversations about possibilities
Therapist is the expert and has special knowledge regarding trauma to which patient submits; therapist gives advice	Client and therapist both have particular areas of expertise; therapist asks questions to elicit client's expertise
Problem is always there	Exceptions to the problem are always there
Long-term treatment	Variable/individualized length of treatment
Treatment aim is recovery from symptoms of PTSD	Treatment aim is what client wants to have instead of symptoms of PTSD: recovery and maybe growth
Coping mechanisms need to be learned	Coping mechanisms are already present
Big changes are needed	Small changes are often enough
Insight or understanding is a precondition	Insight or understanding may come during or after treatment
Exposure therapy is a sine qua non	Exposure therapy may be valuable, but is not a sine qua non

TABLE 3.1 *(Continued)* **Differences in Therapeutic Approaches to Trauma**	
Traditional Approaches to Trauma	**The SF Approach to Trauma**
Feedback (sometimes) from patient at end of therapy	Feedback from client after every session
Therapist defines end of treatment	Client defines end of treatment

The SF approach can replace traditional approaches or may be combined with them. For example, biological treatments seem to be strictly problem-focused. Nevertheless, it makes a difference if clients have the idea that "the depression will disappear" or that they (in positive terms) will become "energetic, active, or relaxed." An SF approach to *pharmacological treatment* may consist of encouraging clients to give a detailed description of what the first signs of recovery might look like, assuming that the medication takes effect, and of how the recovery will further manifest itself. Clients are asked what they themselves can add to the effect of the medication, or what they can do to create an environment in which the medication will have the maximum effect in helping them to pull through (Bakker et al., 2010).

For example, the combination of SFBT and EMDR may be useful. First, invite clients to describe their preferred future and find exceptions to the problem (e.g., intrusions, nightmares, phobic reactions). In addition, suggest that techniques such as exposure or EMDR could be helpful to reach a higher point on the scale, and find out whether clients may be interested in this approach.

From an SF point of view, keeping clients in the *expert position* is important.

To help clients regain control, therapists may say, "Some clients have said it's helpful to explore the past. Some clients have made the changes they wanted first and addressed the traumatic memories later. And there were clients who reached their preferred future and didn't want or need to look back at what happened to them. What do you suppose will be most helpful for you?" Clients can stay in the expert position when therapists ask them what they· already know about trauma treatments or invite them to find (more) information on the Internet. Or therapists may first explain several treatment possibilities (such as exposure therapy, EMDR, or compassion-focused therapy) and then invite clients to reflect on which method they may find most useful. Erickson, the famous psychiatrist–hypnotherapist, often gave clients the choice of two or more alternatives. When alternatives exist, the feelings of choice and freedom are maintained better than in a situation where clients are told exactly what to do.

SF questions in this chapter are:

15. "How have you managed to survive? What helps you deal with what you've experienced?"
16. "What else have you been through that was difficult, and what helped

you then? Which of the things that helped you then could be useful to you again now?"

17. "Do you know anyone else who has been through the same ordeal? What has helped that person deal with it?"

18. "What does it mean for you to have survived these events?" or "What was good about this experience?"

19. "If a miracle were to happen in the middle of the night and you overcame the consequences of these events well enough that you didn't have to come here anymore and were (relatively) satisfied with your life, what would be different then?" or "Supposing you woke up tomorrow and your past was no longer messing with your future, what would be the first sign you'd notice?"

20. "What will you be doing differently when these traumatic memories are less of a problem in your daily life?"

21. "What difference will those healing changes make in your life when they have lasted for a longer period of time (days, weeks, months, years)? What difference will they make in your relationships with important people in your life? What difference will the changes that you've accomplished make for future generations of your family?"

22. "What will be the smallest sign that things are going better? What difference will that make for you? What will be the next smallest sign? And the one after that? How will you be able to tell that you're handling things a little better or that things are a little easier for you?"

23. "How can you regain hope that life can get easier in the future?"

24. "What did the terrible event *not* change, and how did you manage that?

What things in your life do you wish to maintain despite what has happened?"

25. "What helps you keep traumatic images (intrusions) and memories under control?"

26. "On a scale of 10 to 0, where 10 equals you are handling what's happened very well and 0 equals you can't handle what's happened at all, where are you now?" (and follow-up scaling questions).

27. "How do you now manage to sometimes feel safe and have control of your life?"

28. "How can you comfort yourself? Who else can comfort you now, even if only a little bit?"

29. "How do you manage to come out of . . . (the dissociation)?" or "How do you manage to stop hurting yourself? What else helps in this respect?"

30. "How will you celebrate your victory over what happened to you?"

In the next chapter, we will look at how to create a context for change to help clients move on from the aftereffects of trauma to recovery and perhaps posttraumatic growth.

4

Creating a Context for Change

Introduction

In this chapter, the focus is on helping clients move on from the repercussions of trauma to recovery and perhaps to posttraumatic growth. It starts with building *rapport* and creating a positive *alliance*, a necessary condition of change across all forms of psychotherapy. Acknowledgment and validation of clients' experiences are other prerequisites of the therapeutic process. It is important to let clients know that their experiences, their points of view, and their actions have been heard and to normalize and reframe their experiences. Building hope and optimism are important, because most trauma survivors go through very difficult times before they come to see a therapist and feel hopeless and pessimistic about possibilities for change (see Volume 2: Depression).

The Therapeutic Alliance

Psychotherapy starts with building *rapport*. The alliance represents a positive working relationship between therapists and clients as well as active and collaborative engagement of all involved. Therapists should make explicit efforts to facilitate the creation of a positive and strong alliance. They should also systematically monitor the alliance rather than relying on clinical impression (see Chapter 8 and 9). Keep in mind that the client's view of the alliance (and not the therapists'!) is the best predictor of outcome. Attention should be paid to the alliance as soon as therapy begins, because positive early alliance is a good predictor of improvement whereas poor early alliance predicts client dropout.

In SFBT, the alliance is a negotiated, consensual, and cooperative endeavor in which therapists and clients focus on (a) exceptions, (b) goals, and (c) solutions. When clients are motivated to change, SFBT calls this a *customer-relationship*. When clients are mandated and have no personal problem to work on, this is called a *visitor-relationship*. Sometimes clients want someone else or something else to change; SFBT calls this a *complainant-relationship*. If therapists are not on the same page as their clients, clients may use the expression *yes, but*, which therapists often interpret as resistance. *Yes, but* drains energy from the conversation, which soon turns into a discussion that revolves around who is right (for a detailed description of *yes, but* and *yes, and*, see Volume 2: Depression).

Four strategies may be applied in a situation where clients think someone or something else needs to change:

1. Say that you wish you could help them, but that you are not a magician. Say you don't think that anyone is able to change anyone else, so how else might you help them? Or ask them, "How is this a problem for you?"

2. Ask them to imagine the other changing in the desired direction and tell you what they would notice different about him or her. Also ask what they would notice different about themselves and what difference that would make to their relationship;

3. Investigate a future in which the other is not changing by asking clients what they can still do themselves;

4. Figure out the hoped-for outcome behind earlier attempts at change.

EXERCISE 7. COMPLAIN ABOUT A THIRD PERSON

Find a partner to do this exercise with and ask him or her to complain about someone else, a third person (not you!) they would like to change. Ask him or her to talk about the same complaint every time so that you can practice the four different strategies described above. Notice the differences brought about by each strategy. Then change roles. In the role of the client, you can learn a lot from the different types of questions that are asked of you.

Focusing on Change

A focus on change is another prerequisite of the therapeutic process. The most useful way to decide which door can be opened to get solutions is to get a description of what clients will be doing differently and/or what things will be happening that are different when the problem is solved, thus creating the expectation of beneficial change (De Shazer, 1985).

Therapists are constantly reminding clients that they cannot change other people, only themselves. How ironic, therefore, that therapists are trained to develop a treatment plan and enter sessions with the intention of changing their clients!

In SFBT, *the role of therapists* is different. Whereas in traditional forms of psychotherapy, the therapist is the only expert in the room, the one who explores and analyzes the problem and gives advice on how to solve problems, in SFBT the role is one where therapists ask SF questions (they are *not-knowing*), are one step behind their clients, and look in the same direction (toward the client's preferred future). This stance is called *leading from one step behind*. Clients are seen as co-experts; they are invited to share their knowledge and expertise (Bannink, 2007, 2008a, 2010a). When people believe that their personal qualities can be developed further, then despite the pain of failure, they don't become pessimistic, because they are not being defined by their failures. Change and growth remain a possibility, opening up pathways to success. Dweck (2006) found that students with a fixed mindset have stronger complaints than students with a *growth mindset* (see Volume 2: Depression).

Acknowledgment and Validation

Psychotherapy with trauma survivors is impossible if the negative impact a problem has goes unacknowledged. Clients are often in great distress and generally want to make that known. Therapists respectfully listen to their story and shift to a more positive conversation as soon as possible. However, it is a misconception that there can be acknowledgment only if the problem is wholly explored or if clients are afforded every opportunity to expatiate on their view of the problem. Utterances by therapists such as "I understand that this must have been difficult for you" or "I wonder how you have coped so well" offer acknowledgement just as well and take up considerably less time than having clients describe the entire problem. Asking clients what they have tried so far to solve the problem also offers acknowledgement, since most clients have taken steps to address their problems before therapy. However, the SF question "What have you tried so far *that has been helpful, even just a little bit*?" invites clients to talk about successes (however small) instead of the failures that are usually discussed when only the first part of the question is asked.

Validation of the client's point of view is also important: "I am sure you must have a good reason for this." In this way, therapists show that they respect their clients' opinions and ideas. At the beginning of the first session, therapists may give clients one opportunity *to say what definitively needs to be said* before switching to what clients want different in their lives. This has become a proven method in SF conflict management (Bannink, 2008b, 2009b, 2010b).

SF questions for offering acknowledgement and validation are:

- "How do you cope? How do you keep your head above water?"
- "How do you ensure the situation isn't worse than it is? How do you do that? Which personal strengths and resources do you use?"

STORY 6. ACKNOWLEDGE THE PROBLEM

Long ago, the inhabitants of a village were starving because they were afraid of a dragon in their fields. One day a traveler came to the village and asked for food. The villagers explained that they didn't dare to harvest their crops because they were afraid of this dragon. When the traveler heard their story, he offered to slay the dragon, but arriving at the fields he saw only a large watermelon. He said to the villagers that they had nothing to fear because there was no dragon, only a watermelon. The villagers were angry at his refusal to understand their fear and hacked him to pieces.

Another traveler came passing by the village, and he too offered to slay the dragon, much to the relief of the villagers. But they hacked him to pieces as well, because he too said they were mistaken about the dragon.

In the meantime the villagers were desperate, but then a third traveler came to the village. He too promised to kill the dragon. He saw the giant watermelon, reflected for a moment, drew his sword, and hacked the watermelon to pieces. He returned to the village and told the people he had killed their dragon. The traveler stayed in the village, long enough to teach the villagers the difference between dragons and watermelons.

When clients and/or therapists think that they (or their clients, in the case of therapists) need to work through trauma or need to talk about what happened, they are telling us that they have a *theory of change* about what will help. When the invitation into these often problem-saturated conversations is accepted, SF therapists look for and initiate opportunities to help clients identify what changes they hope will result from talking about these experiences (in terms of solutions and goals; George, 2010).

SF questions for clients to ask themselves in order to *alter their theory of change* are:

- "How will talking about these experiences be helpful in making the changes I want?"
- "How will I know that we have talked enough about these experiences so I can concentrate more on where I would like to go rather than where I've been?"
- "What will be the first signs that will tell me that I'm putting the past behind me?"

Normalizing and Reframing

Normalizing is used to depathologize clients' concerns and present them instead as normal life difficulties. It helps clients to calm down and realize they're not abnormal for having this problem. Thinking it's not normal to have a problem causes a further problem. People are more compassionate with themselves and experience lower negative affect when they see that others have the same problems they have.

It is advisable, whenever possible, to normalize and neutralize both the problem itself and the ways in which clients and their environment respond to it. Neutral language is essential; accusations, threats, hurtful speech, and other words with negative emotional connotations must be avoided. Normalization puts clients at ease, changes the moral judgment of and by other persons, and encourages greater understanding from and of the other.

It is important to keep in mind that the clients *are* not the problem, but that they are individuals who *have* a problem. Labels like "depressed" or "borderline" are best avoided. After all, the client is much more than his or her problem or diagnosis. Instead of saying, "Cindy is a borderliner," say, "Cindy has a borderline personality disorder." O'Hanlon and Rowan (2003) also emphasize the importance of *distinguishing between the person and the illness* and of examining the effects of the illness on the person. Ask not what disease the person has, but rather what person the disease has. Reframing traumatic experiences in terms of survivorship and heroism rather than victimization may also be helpful (see Exercise 30, pgs. 139-140).

CASE 5. NOBODY CAN UNDERSTAND
WHAT I'VE BEEN THROUGH

The client had suffered sexual abuse by her father as a child. Later in life she developed symptoms of PTSD: numbness, nightmares, and sexual problems with her boyfriend. She never talked about her experiences because she thought, "Nobody can understand what I've been through." The therapist invited her to think about the following: "Supposing someone could understand, what difference would that make for me? What would be different in my life? What else would be different?"

The client thought that she would feel less alone and more connected to the world. She would go out more and try to talk with her boyfriend about what had happened to her. At that point she realized that, although her boyfriend might never understand completely what she had been through, she could start sharing her experiences with him just the same.

Building Hope

The interest in hope in psychotherapy was initially aimed at reducing despair rather than increasing hopeful thoughts. Given the link between despair and suicide, A. T. Beck, Weissman, Lester, and Trexles (1974) focused on combating hopelessness. Their definition of hopelessness was a system of cognitive schemas whose common denomination is negative expectations about the future.

In *crisis situations*, the available time does not usually lend itself to an elaborate diagnosis, and clients in crisis benefit from regaining confidence in their personal competencies and a future-oriented approach, building positive expectations instead of negative ones. Think of questions such as "How do you manage to carry on?" or "What has helped you in the past weeks, even if only slightly?" Commonly, clients in crisis relinquish competence to the therapist ("You tell me what I should do")—a pitfall that can be avoided using SFBT.

The mere willingness to take part in a conversation with a therapist generates hope and positive expectancy. These are strengthened when clients' attention is directed toward their options rather than limitations. When therapists steer clients' attention to their *previous successes* instead of failures, a further positive expectancy is generated. The notion of the client's personal control is emphasized and problems may be placed outside the client, which serves to remove blame from them. If, however, therapists have no confidence in their ability to help clients reach their goals and have lost hope of a favorable outcome, they should examine what is needed to regain hope. Or they should turn clients over to a more hopeful colleague. It is often the assumptions, the attitude, and the behavior of therapists themselves that lead to hopeless cases (see Chapter 8).

STORY 7. UPWARD SPIRAL OF HOPE

There are two basic responses to hardship: despair and hope. In despair, negativity is multiplied. Fear and uncertainty turn into stress, which can change into hopeless sadness or shame. Despair smothers all forms of positivity, and connections with others are lost. Despair opens the gate to a downward spiral. Hope is different. It is not the mirror reflection of despair. Hope acknowledges negativity with clear eyes and kindles positivity, allowing people to connect with others. Hope opens the gateway to an upward spiral to bounce back from hardship and emerge even stronger and more resourceful than before. Hope is the belief that the future will be better than today (this belief is the same as in optimism) *and* the belief that an individual can influence this.

The protection *hope* gives in coping with trauma has been exemplified by various spiritual models, from Moses, Jesus, and Muhammad to Martin Luther King. Hope as a positive psychological strength may be a universal resource for positive adaptations and changes. Frank and Frank (1991, p. 132) looked at the elements of hope in medical treatments. "Hopelessness can retard recovery or hasten death, while mobilizing hope plays an important part in many forms of healing. Favorable expectations generate feelings of optimism, energy, and well-being and may actually promote

PTG

healing, especially of those illnesses that have a large psychological or emotional component."

A way to enhance hope is to tell clients stories about people in similar situations who have overcome hardship. This helps clients identify the positive steps they have taken this far and helps them identify the positive aspects of the situation. More SF questions about hope and optimism are described in Volume 1: Anxiety and Volume 2: Depression.

STORY 8. POSITIVE CHANGES IN KOSOVAR WAR REFUGEES

Research on war trauma has been dominated by a pathological focus for decades. However, researchers have now counterbalanced previous studies of trauma with a new focus: positive changes following crisis. Ai, Tice, Whitsett, Ishisaka, and Chim (2007) examined how specific psychological factors influenced postwar adaptive outcomes in a sample of 50 Kosovar war refugees. The Kosovars in this study were not soldiers but victims of the severe sociopolitical and economic consequences of war. Undergoing an abrupt relocation directly from the war zone and leaving everything behind, they brought fresh wounds from brutal experiences in relation to the Serbian–Albanian conflict, NATO bombing, retributive persecution, and ethnic cleansing. The researchers explored individual differences in positive attitude and coping strategies. The found that hope assessed during resettlement and cognitive coping strategies employed between resettlement and follow-up were associated with post traumatic growth (PTG). Ai et al. (2007) concluded that future mental health practice with refugees should address both positive and negative aspects.

Many therapists feel anxious when talking with clients who are feeling hopeless and thinking of *committing suicide*. Their initial impulse may be to persuade them that suicide is not the right option. However, by contradicting them, they may isolate their clients even further. Another reaction of therapists is to minimize or refuse to believe what may be the client's desperate cry for help. Or they think all suicidal clients should be hospitalized and use medication.

The best way to feel hopeful about clients' prospects is to keep in mind that clients who are talking about suicide are still alive for some reason and to invite them to think about how they are still surviving. Coping questions and competence questions are important in (re)gaining a glimmer of hope.

SF questions in *crisis situations* are:

- "How did you manage to get out of bed this morning? Compared to other (bad) days, what did you do differently this morning that helped you get up and come here?"
- "How have you been able to hold on long enough to come here?"
- "How did you manage for so long without seeking professional help?"

- "What are you doing to take care of yourself in this situation?"
- "What is the most important thing for you to remember to continue to cope with this situation?"
- "What would you like to be different when this is over?"
- "How will you/others notice that you have overcome the crisis?"
- "Suppose a miracle happens tonight, and the miracle is that you can cope with this difficult situation, but you are unaware that the miracle has happened because you are asleep. What will you notice first thing tomorrow morning that shows you that the miracle has happened? What else will be different? When the miracle occurs, what will take the place of your pain and your thoughts of killing yourself?"
- "When was the last time you ate something? How did you manage to do that? How did that help you?" "When was the last time you slept? How did you manage to do that? How did that help you?"
- "What helped in the past, even if only marginally?"
- "How do you cope with everything that is going on and all you have gone through?"
- "How do you succeed in getting from one moment to the next?"
- "How will you get through the rest of the day?"
- "When do you not have these (e.g., suicidal) thoughts?"
- "Is there anyone else who shares this with you? How is that helpful?"
- "What do your friends or family say you do well, even in very bad times?"
- "Suppose there is a solution. What difference will that make? What will be different, and, more specifically, what will be better?"

- "Some trauma survivors depend on others for hope, because they feel hopeless and must rely on *borrowed hope*—hope that others hold out for them. What are important people in your life hoping for? What are their best hopes for you?"

- "Suppose you look back 1 year, 5 years, or 10 years from now. What will you see that has helped you emerge from this crisis?" or "Suppose that 1 year, 5 years, or 10 years from now you look back together with a friend. What do both of you say you have done in the preceding year(s) that has helped you come out of this so well?"

- "What do you think is the most useful thing that I can do at this moment?"

CASE 6. GIVING UP ALL HOPE OF HAVING A BETTER PAST

Hope is always future-oriented; one cannot hope for something to happen in the past. However, sometimes people keep on hoping that the past were different. For example, clients who have experienced a difficult childhood may ruminate upon how they would have liked things to be different. One client kept on saying how he wished his mother had been a warm and caring person instead of the cold person she actually had been. The therapist acknowledged his feelings and asked him to reflect on the following question: "How will I know when I am ready and able *to give up all hope of having a better past*?"

PTG

STORY 9. I WILL PREVAIL

Hope is strongly linked to optimism. More than 30 Vietnam war veterans who had been held as prisoners of war for six to eight years while being tortured and kept in solitary confinement were interviewed and tested. Unlike fellow veterans, they did not develop depression or PTSD after their release, even though they had endured extreme stress. What was their secret? Ten characteristics set them apart, the top one being optimism ("I am in a tough spot, but I will prevail"). Other characteristics included having strong social support (they used a tapping system on the walls to keep in contact with each other), altruism, humor, and the feeling that life had meaning and that they had something to live for (Charney, 2012).

Another way to install hope is to ask clients about *pretreatment change* (see Chapter 2): "Many clients notice that, between the time they call for an appointment and the first session, things already seem different. What have you noticed about your situation?" or "Since you made the appointment and our session today, what is better (even just a little bit)? What are these positive changes saying about you as a person?"

Scheduling an appointment may help set the wheel of change in motion and present the possibility for an emergent story of competence and mastery. This is consistent with the SF supposition that everything is subject to change and that the point is not to find out *whether* useful change takes place but *when* useful change takes or has taken place.

SF questions in this chapter are:

31. "How is this a problem for you?"
32. "Imagine the other person changing in the direction desired. What would you notice different about him? What would you notice different about yourself? What difference would that make to your relationship? At what moment is this already occurring?"
33. "What have you tried so far that has been helpful, even just a little bit?"
34. "How do you cope? How do you keep your head above water?"
35. "How do you ensure the situation isn't worse than it is? Which personal strengths and resources do you use?"
36. "How do you suppose talking about these experiences will be helpful in making the changes you want? How will you know (what will be the signs that tell you) that we have talked enough about these experiences so we can concentrate more on where you would like to go rather than where you've been?"
37. "What will be the first signs that will tell you that you're putting the past behind you?"
38. "How did you manage to come here?" or "How did you manage to get out of bed this morning? Compared to other (bad) days, what did you do differently this morning that helped you get up and come here?"

39. "How have you been able to hold on long enough to come here?" or "How did you manage for so long without seeking professional help?"

40. "What are you doing to take care of yourself in this situation? What is the most important thing for you to remember to continue to cope with this situation?"

41. "What would you like to be different when this is over? How will you/ others notice that you have overcome the crisis? Suppose a miracle happens tonight, and the miracle is that you can cope with this situation, but you are unaware that the miracle has happened because you were asleep. What will you notice first thing tomorrow morning that will show you that the miracle has taken place? What else will be different? When this miracle occurs, what will take the place of your pain and thoughts of killing yourself?"

42. "When was the last time you ate something? When was the last time you slept? How did you manage to do that? How did that help you?"

43. "What helped in the past, even if only marginally?"

44. "How do you cope with everything that is going on and all you have gone through? How do you succeed in getting from one moment to the next?"

45. "How will you get through the rest of the day?"

46. "When do you not have these (e.g., suicidal) thoughts?"

47. "Is there anyone else who shares this with you? How is that helpful?"

48. "What do your friends or family say you do well, even in very bad times?"

49. "Suppose there is a solution. What difference will that make? What will be different—and, more specifically, better?"

50. "Some survivors depend on others for hope, because they feel hopeless and must rely on *borrowed hope*—hope that others hold out for them. What are important people in your life hoping for? What are their best hopes for you?"

51. "Suppose you look back 1 year, 5 years, or 10 years from now. What will you see that has helped you emerge from this crisis?" or "Suppose that 1 year, 5 years, or 10 years from now you look back together with a friend. What do both of you say you have done in the preceding year or years that has helped you come out of this so well?"

52. "What do you think is the most useful thing that I can do at this moment?"

53. "Many clients notice that, between the time they call for an appointment and the first session, things already seem different. What have you noticed about your situation?" or "Since you made the appointment and our session today, what is better (even just a little bit)? What are these positive changes saying about you as a person?"

In the next chapter, we will see how the invitation to describe their preferred future helps clients to focus on possibilities rather than on problems.

5

Describing the Preferred Future

Introduction

How people see their future influences how they behave today. Therefore, investing in the future pays off today. The good news is that people can edit the stories about their future self. The invitation to describe a new life (De Shazer, 1991, p. 122) focuses on possibilities rather than on problems and emphasizes the possibility of change.

Setting a goal helps to impose structure on treatment. It also makes explicit that therapy will be terminated when the goal is achieved, or will be discontinued if there is little or no progress. It also provides the opportunity for an evaluation of outcome. This chapter explained how to set a well-defined goal by inviting clients to give a detailed description of their preferred future, often using future-oriented techniques.

Clients may also be invited to change their perspectives, which can be done in several ways: by changing the meaning of what has happened, by asking relationship questions, by externalizing the problem, or by using a spiritual perspective. (Using a third-person perspective is another way to change perspective; this is described in Volume 1: Anxiety.) Once clients have described their new lives, an assessment of motivation, hope, and confidence is made.

STORY 10. THE CHESHIRE CAT

The Cheshire Cat is a fictional cat popularized by Lewis Carroll's depiction of it in *Alice's Adventures in Wonderland* (1865). The cat is known for its distinctive mischievous grin. Alice encounters the Cheshire Cat outside on the branches of a tree, where it appears and disappears at will.

Alice: Would you tell me, please, which way I ought to go from here?
The Cat: That depends a good deal on where you want to get to.
Alice: I don't much care where.
The Cat: Then it doesn't much matter which way you go.

Setting a Well-Defined Goal

When a man doesn't know what harbor he is making for, no wind is the right wind (Seneca, 2011). If therapists do not know where they are heading with their clients, they will probably end up in the wrong place. Often therapists have taken on the responsibility of setting goals for clients rather than allowing clients to sort out goals for themselves. SFBT always aims for the client's goal, not that of their therapists.

In problem-focused therapies, it is assumed that the problem is blocking clients from being able to move forward toward their goal. It is assumed that once the problem is solved, clients can move forward in a more productive direction. The way that clients and therapists typically agree to know that the problem is solved is when the problem is reduced or gone: Clients are no longer depressed, or no longer use drugs or alcohol. However, if psychotherapy focuses solely on the reduction of the undesired situation, clients might not yet have replaced it with the desired situation. Finishing therapy at a point where something is not happening rather than at a point when the preferred future is happening has a greater risk of relapse. Bannink (2014b) describes several suggestions for setting well-defined goals (see Volume 1: Anxiety). The majority of SF conversations focus on three interrelated activities (De Shazer, 1991):

1. Producing exceptions—examples of the goal(s) in clients' lives that point to desired changes
2. Imagining and describing clients' new lives
3. Confirming that change is occurring and that clients' new lives have indeed started

CASE 7. TAXI DRIVER

I sometimes explain to clients and colleagues that my work is comparable to that of a *taxi driver*. Clients define the destination of the taxi ride (the goal) and it is my responsibility to drive them safely there, ensuring that the route is as short as possible and the ride is comfortable. My first question—as a taxi driver—is "Where to?" instead of "Where from?" If the clients answers "Not the airport" ("I don't want this problem"), I ask where he or she would like to go instead (Bannink & McCarthy, 2014).

SF questions for setting a well-defined goal are:

- "What is the purpose of your visit?"
- "What will be the best outcome of your coming to see me?"
- "What would you like to have accomplished by the end of this session (or these sessions) in order for you to say that it has been useful?"
- "What will indicate to you/others that you don't need to come back anymore?"
- "What would you/others like to see different as a result of these sessions?"
- "What are your best hopes? What difference will it make when your best hopes are met?"
- "Suppose you're asleep tonight and a miracle happens. The miracle is

that the problem that brings you here has been solved (to a sufficient degree). You are unaware of this, however, because you are asleep. What will you notice first thing tomorrow morning that indicates the problem has been solved? What will be different? What will you be doing differently? How else will you notice over the course of the day that the miracle has happened? How else? How will others notice that the miracle has occurred? How will they react differently?"

- "How would your life look if you were not (depressed/anxious/angry)?" or "Who would you be without the trauma?"
- "Supposing there were a miracle pill with only positive side effects, how would your life be different?"
- "What *impossible* goal could you reach if you completely ignored your limitations?"
- "Let's image you are at your best. What will you be doing that shows that you are at your best?"

great ex

CASE 8. THE MIRACLE QUESTION

The client is asked the *miracle question*. He describes the unrealistic situation in which both parents, who died a few years before, are still alive. Only then would he no longer feel lonely and listless; he would be joyful and feel happy again. The SF therapist acknowledges the client's sorrow and asks a hypothetical question: "Suppose your parents were still alive. What would be different in your life?" The client says he would have a place where he felt safe and someone who cared about him. The therapist asks, "What difference would it make for you to have a safe place and the sense that someone cares about you?" Then: "In what situations do you have a sense of safety and the sense that someone cares about you, even just a little bit?" The client answers that this used to be the case with his only sister. However, in the wake of an argument lately, he has seen little of her. After he calls her, the relationship slowly begins to improve.

Even if clients put forward an unrealistic goal, SF therapists examine with them what this would mean for them and what possibilities there are to attain at least a realistic part of their preferred future.

Future-Oriented Techniques

SFBT starts with the detailed description of the clients' new lives: what they choose to become. They are invited to do some *therapeutic time traveling*. Future-oriented techniques use their inner wisdom: Clients usually already know the solution(s) to the problem, only they do not know (yet) that they know. More future-oriented techniques are described in Volume 1: Anxiety.

Erickson (1954) was one of the first psychotherapists to use a future-oriented technique, called *pseudo-orientation in time*. During hypnosis, he had clients imagine running into him in six months and telling him that the problem had been solved and how they had achieved that. And even though they did not always apply the same solutions that they had put forward, it turned out that many of them reported doing better six months later.

Imagining a *best possible self* is useful in goal-setting and building hope and optimism. For 20 minutes on four consecutive days, participants in a study done by King (2001) were asked to write down their ideal future, in which all had gone well and they had met their hopes and goals (using the exercise *best possible self,* see below). Another group was asked to write about a traumatic experience for those minutes on four consecutive days. Yet another group was asked to write about their ideal future as well as the trauma. The last group was asked to just write about their plans for the day on those four days. The results were that writing about life goals was significantly less upsetting than writing about trauma and was associated with a significant increase in well-being. Five months after writing, a significant interaction emerged such that writing about the ideal future and writing about the trauma were both associated with decreased illness compared to the other two groups.

EXERCISE 8. BEST POSSIBLE SELF

Invite clients to imagine a future in which they are bringing their *best possible self* forward. Ask them to visualize a best possible self that is very pleasing to them and whom they are interested in. Also ask them to imagine that they have worked hard and succeeded at

accomplishing their life goals. You might think of this as the realization of their life dreams and of their own best potential. The point is
not to think of unrealistic fantasies, but rather things that are positive and attainable. After they get a clear description, invite them
to write the details down. Writing down thoughts and hopes helps
one move from the realm of foggy ideas and fragmented thoughts
to concrete, real possibilities.

EXERCISE 9. LETTER FROM YOUR FUTURE

Invite clients to write a letter *from* their future self *to* their current self from *X* years from now (6 months, 1 year, 5 years, or maybe
10 years, whichever is for them a relevant period of time; Dolan,
1991). Ask them to describe how they are doing fine, where they are,
what they are doing, and what crucial things they have realized or
done to get there. Finally ask them to give their present selves some
sage and compassionate advice from the future.

Yet another future-oriented technique, *older and wiser self,* invites clients to imagine that many years later they are an *older and wiser version of
themselves* (Dolan, 1991). They are still healthy and have all their intellectual
capabilities. Clients may even go for a walk with the older and wiser version
and ask for advice regarding their problem:

- "What would this older and wise person advise me to do in order to get through the present phase of my life?"
- "What would this person say I should be thinking of?"
- "What would this person say that would help me the best to recover from the past and function well (again)?"
- "What would this person say about how I can console myself?"
- "How, from this person's view, could therapy (if needed) be most useful to me?"

STORY 11. TOP PERFORMERS

How do top performers set goals? Barrell, a performance improvement expert working with baseball players, stated that there are "toward goals" and "away goals." Which one you use has quite an impact on performance. Toward goals have you visualize and create connections around where you are going. You are creating new connections in your brain. What is interesting is that you start to feel good at lower levels with toward goals. There are benefits earlier. Away goals have you visualize what can go wrong, which reactivates the negative emotions involved (Barrell & Ryback, 2008).

Top performers review the details of their performance, identifying specific actions and alternate strategies for reaching their goals. Whereas unsuccessful people attribute failure to external and uncontrollable factors ("I just had a bad day"), successful people more often cite controllable factors ("I should have done this instead of that"). Mediocre therapists are likelier to spend time hypothesizing about failed strategies—believing that understanding the reasons why an approach did not work will lead to better outcomes—and less time thinking about strategies that might be more effective.

CASE 9. ONCE AND FOR ALL

The client asks, "How will I know I have *once and for all* resolved the trauma of being raped when I was 14 years old?" The therapist answers, "You may say you have resolved the trauma when you can continue with your life, without suffering from symptoms such as depression, flashbacks or nightmares *and* when you have what you feel is a sufficient level of well-being. Having resolved the trauma in a good way, however, is not the same as *finally* having resolved the trauma. If later in life you go through a similar experience, chances are that memories of the first trauma will, perhaps temporarily, return." The therapist then suggests using the metaphor of the client's brain as a library (see Exercise 10).

EXERCISE 10. YOUR BRAIN AS A LIBRARY

Invite clients to think of the metaphor of their *brain as a library*. The books close to the entrance contain the pleasant and unpleasant things that have happened to them recently. Books containing what happened earlier in their life are placed on the shelves, which are more to the back of the library (and may even have gathered some dust). Invite clients to imagine they are the librarian. They can move the books according to what they think is wise and helpful. If a book containing an unpleasant event shows up every time at the front of the library, ask them to move the book to the shelves at the back and put some books with pleasant events toward the front. Invite them to repeat this a couple of times. In this way, they may become the director of their thoughts.

It may be helpful for clients to ask their therapists the following question at the start of therapy: "How shall I view my past once we are finished here?" Another way to describe a new life opens up when therapists invite clients to *construct the history of their solutions*—before the change actually takes place (George, 2010). This often takes a shorter route than talking about the past is likely to take. Invite clients to ask themselves:

- "Looking back, what has it taken to make the changes that I have made?"
- "When in the past have I seen myself drawing on those qualities in a way that is useful to me?"
- "Having made these changes, looking back to the time before the change, what tells me that I always did have the capacity to make these changes?"
- "Of all those who have known me in my past, who would be least surprised by the changes I have made? And what is it that those people knew about me and my possibilities that others perhaps didn't?"

Using Different Perspectives

Inviting clients to change their perspective can be done in several ways. They may be invited to *change the meaning* of what happened to them. Another way to change perspective is to construct descriptions of interactional events and their meaning by asking *relationship questions*. The third way is to *externalize the problem*: Clients are invited to see the problem as something separate from themselves that affects them, but does not always control every aspect of their lives. The fourth way is to use a *spiritual perspective*. These perspectives are described below. Using the *third-person perspective* is described in Volume 1: Anxiety.

Traumatic experiences cannot change, no matter what clients do in relation to them in therapy. All that can change is the *meaning* that these events have in the present and the expectation of the meaning that they will have in the future. This struggle in *finding meaning* is the crucible of growth at the core of cognitive–emotional processing after trauma (Joseph & Linley, 2005).

One way to shift meaning is to talk about the events themselves. For example, in working with survivors of sexual abuse, the shift from the idea that it was their fault that the abuse happened to the idea that it wasn't their fault has a big impact on the lives of many clients. However, a shift of meaning can often be achieved without talking about the trauma (George, 2010). As clients and therapists move forward, clients develop more confidence that the future will be satisfactory. In making this shift, the meaning of the trauma has been changed from an event that is minute by minute determining the client's life to an event that happened, one that should not have happened, and yet one that is no longer controlling the client. The event has been _detoxified_. Two questions for inviting clients to think in this direction are:

1. "How will I know that what happened is no longer holding me back in my life?"
2. "How will I know that I am doing justice to myself and my possibilities despite what was done to me?"

EXERCISE 11. DETOXIFY TRAUMATIC EXPERIENCES

When clients suffering from PTSD are invited to draw a circle and then to draw a point that represents the most traumatic experience in their life, they often draw this point right in the middle of the circle, symbolic for the central place the event plays in their lives. Therapists ask whether putting the event in this central place is helpful, or would clients rather have the point a bit less central in a better future? For each point clients choose, therapists ask what difference that makes for them and important others. Therapists may also ask about helpful exceptions and how clients are/were able to bring them about.

When using *relationship questions*, therapists find out who the clients' significant others are and weave them into the questions so as to encourage clients to describe their situation and what they want different in interactional terms: "Supposing the two of you got along better in the future, what would he notice you doing instead of losing your temper?" or "What will your children say will be different when things are somewhat better?"

Walter and Peller (1992) introduced the interactional matrix, a tool for building solutions from an interactional view to invite clients into areas of difference (see Figure 5.1). Across the top of the matrix are the following frames: Goal, Hypothetical Solutions, and Exceptions. Along the left side of the matrix are the different reporting positions. The first is the *for self* position. Questions from this position invite clients to answer from their own point of view. The next position is *for the other*. Questions from this position invite clients to answer questions as if they were listening and reporting for someone else. In order to answer these questions, clients have to suspend their own way of thinking and imagine the other person answering the question. They have to put themselves in the other's shoes or at least think of what the other person might say if he or she were responding to the question.

The third row of the matrix reports from a *detached position (observer)*. This position is that of someone observing: "If I were a fly on the wall observing you and your partner, what would I see you doing differently when things are better?" Each question or row of the matrix invites clients into an area of experience different from their usual way of thinking.

FIGURE 5.1 **Interactional Matrix**			
Position	**Goals**	**Hypothetical solutions**	**Exceptions**
Self			
Other			
Observer			

EXERCISE 12. INTERACTIONAL MATRIX

Do this exercise with a colleague or partner. Think of a situation where you have a problem with another person (not your colleague or partner!). Keep the same order: from goal to hypothetical solutions/miracle to exceptions. Notice the differences in your reactions and how this changes your personal film. Then choose the next row with another viewpoint and notice again how this changes your reaction. What differences do you notice in your personal film? Which questions are most useful to you?

CASE 10. SUPPOSE THERE MIGHT BE SOME WAY FORWARD

After a serious incident at work in which a colleague was killed, the client, who works in an iron factory, expresses his belief that his work is too dangerous and that the atmosphere at work is deteriorating and beyond repair. He has no plans to return to work. Because of the situation, he stays at home, claiming sickness benefits. The therapist asks, "Supposing there might be some way forward, what would be different in your life?" The therapist also asks relationship questions:

- "What would your wife notice you doing differently that would allow her to say you are making progress (*other position*)?"
- "If I were a fly on the wall and I could see that there still remained a faint hope of finding a way forward, what would I see (*detached position*)?"

EXERCISE 13. SELF, OTHER, AND OBSERVER

Ask clients the following *relationship questions* using the same three perspectives (self, other, and observer). These questions may be useful especially in cases where clients want someone else to change. Note that the question starts with "when" instead of "if," suggesting that the problem will (eventually) be solved (see Chapter 2).

1. "When this problem is solved, what will you notice that is different about the other person? What will you see him/her doing differently? What else?"
2. "When this problem is solved, what will this other person notice that is different about you? What will this other person see you doing differently? What else?"
3. "When this problem is solved and an outside observer is watching you, what will he or she notice that is different about your relationship with the other person? What will this observer see both of you doing differently? What else?"

EXERCISE 14. FIND MEANING AND PURPOSE

Having something meaningful to look forward to every day fulfills the human need to make a meaningful contribution to one's life and the lives of others. Invite clients to do something simple every day, such as expressing appreciation of others with a smile, a touch, or a compliment; or making something for the volunteer gift shop; or just calling someone to say hello.

Externalizing the problem helps clients to change perspectives and see the problem as something separate from themselves that affects them but does not always control their lives. This intervention comes from _narrative therapy_ (White & Epston, 1990). With externalization of the problem, clients are free to separate themselves from their problematic self-image. Clients first give a name to the problem, like _Depression_, _Tension_, or _Trauma_: a noun (X) is best for this. "What would you name the problem that bothers you?" Then questions are asked about exceptions—times when X is not there or is less acute—and what clients do to bring that about. Clients are also asked to talk about the times when X is present and how they succeed in coping with it. Depending on their needs, more or less time can be spent on finding out how X controls their lives. Their competencies are highlighted, thus increasing their confidence that more control is possible Also, the tendency to assign blame for the problem to other(s) is minimized. During each session, clients indicate on a scale of 10 to 0 the extent to which X has control over them: 10 equals they have complete control over X and 0 equals X has complete control over them. It is apparent that in most cases the problem may disappear as control over X increases.

SF questions for *externalizing the problem* are:

- "What would you name the problem that is bothering you?"
- "On what point on the scale 10 to 0 are you today?" If the point is higher than last session: "How did you succeed in doing that?" If the point is the same as last session: "How did you manage to maintain the same point?" If the point is lower than last session: "What did you do earlier on to go ahead again? What have you done in the past in a similar situation that has been successful? What have significant others in your life noticed about you in the last week? How did that influence their behavior toward you?"
- "What do you do (differently) when you have (more) control over *X*?"
- "What do you do when you attack *X*? Which weapons help the most?"
- "How are you able to fool or deceive *X*?"
- "How will you celebrate your victory over *X*?"
- "How may you become friends with *X*?"

The <u>fourth</u> way to change perspectives is to use a <u>*spiritual perspective*</u>. O'Hanlon (1999) describes the <u>three C's</u> of spirituality as sources of resilience. <u>*Connection*</u> means moving beyond your little, isolated ego or personality into connection with something bigger, within or outside yourself. <u>*Compassion*</u> means softening your attitude toward yourself or others by aligning with, rather than being against, yourself, others, or the world. And <u>*contribution*</u> means giving unselfish service to others or the world.

STORY 12. A BUDDHIST TALE

A long time ago in India, there lived a young woman named Kisa. She met a man whom she fell in love with and who also loved her. They married and had a son. They were very happy, watching their son grow. However, at the age of two, he suddenly fell ill and died. Kisa's world collapsed. She was overcome by grief so strong that she denied his death altogether. She wandered around, carrying her dead son and asking people desperately for a medicine that would cure him. Eventually she found her way to the Buddha and asked him to cure her son. The Buddha said with deep compassion, "I will help you, but I need a fistful of mustard seeds." When Kisa told him that she was willing to do anything to get the mustard seeds, the Buddha added, "The seeds must be from a house where no one has lost his or her child, spouse, or parents. All the seeds have to be from a house that hasn't been visited by death."

Kisa went from house to house, but in every house the reply was, "We do have mustard seeds, but there are fewer of us alive than dead. Everyone had lost a father or a mother, a wife or a husband, a son or a daughter." Kisa visited many houses and heard many different stories of loss. After she had visited all the houses in the village, she realized that no one is safe from loss and grief and that she wasn't alone. Her grief turned into compassion for the

other grieving people. Then she was able to grieve the death of her
son and bury his body.

—FURMAN, 1998

Assessing Motivation, Hope, and Confidence

It would be nice if clients and therapists could begin with the assumption
that therapy is being used as intended: to find solutions or to put something
behind them. However, not all clients see themselves as being part of the
problem and/or solution. In these cases, traditional psychotherapies use
the concepts of *resistance* and *noncompliance*. Resistance implies that clients
don't want to change and that therapists are separate from the client system
they are treating. However, it is more helpful to see clients as always cooperating: They are showing therapists how they think change takes place. As
therapists understand their thinking and act accordingly, there is always
cooperation. If therapists see resistance in the other person, they cannot
see his or her efforts to cooperate; if, on the other hand, they see his or
her unique way of cooperating, they cannot see resistance. Each new client should be viewed from a position of therapist–client cooperation rather
than from a focus on resistance, power, and control (De Shazer, 1984, p.
13). Clients who do not carry out the homework aren't demonstrating resistance, but are actually cooperating because in that way they are indicating
that this homework is not in accordance with their way of doing things. It

is the therapist's task to assist clients in discovering their competencies and using them to create the preferred future:

> With resistance as a central concept, therapist and client are like opposing tennis players. They are engaged in fighting against each other, and the therapist needs to win in order for the therapy to succeed. With cooperation as a central concept, therapist and client are like tennis players on the same side of the net. Cooperating is a necessity, although sometimes it becomes necessary to fight alongside your partner so that you can cooperatively defeat your mutual opponent.

In Erickson's view also (Rossi, 1980), resistance is cooperative; it is one of the possible responses clients make to interventions.

SF questions in this chapter are:

54. "What is the purpose of your visit?" or "What will be the best outcome of your coming to see me?"
55. "What would you like to have accomplished by the end of this session (or these sessions) in order for you to say that it has been useful?"
56. "What will indicate to you/others that you don't need to come back anymore?"
57. "What would you/others like to see different as a result of these sessions?"

58. "What are your best hopes? What difference will it make when your best hopes are met?"

59. "Suppose you're asleep tonight and a miracle happens. The miracle is that the problem that brings you here has been solved (to a sufficient degree). You are unaware of this, however, because you are asleep. What will you notice first thing tomorrow morning that indicates the problem has been solved? What will be different? What will you be doing differently? How else will you notice over the course of the day that the miracle has happened? How else? How will others notice that the miracle has occurred? How will they react differently?"

60. "How would your life look if you were not . . . (depressed/anxious/angry)?" or "Who would you be without the trauma?"

61. "Supposing there were a miracle pill with only positive side effects, how would your life be different?" or "What *impossible* goal could you reach if you completely ignored your limitations?"

62. "Let's imagine you are at your best. What will you be doing that shows that you are at your best?"

63. "If I were a fly on the wall observing you and your partner, what would I see you doing differently when things are better? What would your wife say you are doing differently that allows her to say you are making progress (*other position*)?"

64. "If I were a fly on the wall and I could still see a faint hope of finding a way forward, what would I see you doing (differently) (*detached position*)?"

65. "When this problem is solved, what will you notice is different about the other person? What will you see him or her doing differently? What else? When this problem is solved, what will this other person notice that is different about you? What will this other person see you doing differently? What else? When this problem is solved and an outside observer is watching you, what will he or she notice that is different about your relationship with the other person? What will this observer see both of you doing differently? What else?"

66. "What would you name the problem that bothers you?" (and all the follow-up scaling questions).

In the next chapter, we will see that all clients possess strengths and competencies that can help to improve the quality of their lives and their well-being. Finding competence helps in discovering how clients manage to cope, even in the most difficult circumstances.

6

Finding Competence

Introduction

Shining a spotlight on change illuminates clients' existing strengths and resources. Erickson (in Rosen, 1991) describes this as clients' *vast storehouse of learning*. Despite life's struggles, all clients possess strengths and competencies that help to improve the quality of their lives and their well-being. Focusing on strengths and competence—making a *success analysis*—increases clients' motivation and helps them to discover how they manage to survive, even in the most difficult circumstances.

Another way to find competence is to find *exceptions*, which clients often overlook. Problems may persist only because clients think or say that the problem "always" occurs. Times when the problem is absent or less of an issue lie at the surface, but they are dismissed as insignificant or are not even noticed and hence remain hidden. SF therapists keep an eye out for exceptions; the interventions are aimed at helping clients to shift their attention to those times when things are/were different and through which solutions reveal themselves.

Asking *competence questions* stimulates clients to talk about successes and positive differences and to give themselves compliments, which feeds their feeling of self-worth. Competence questions are: "How do/did you do that?" "How do/did you manage to . . . ?" "How do you keep going?" Questions about details are key: "What else?" "And what else?" It is important to keep inquiring about everything that looks like a success, a resource, or something that clients value in themselves. Moreover, the question "What else?" implies that there *is* more and that all clients need to do is find out what it is.

Finding Strengths and Resources

All people have capacities that can be drawn upon to better the quality of their life despite the challenges they face. Therapists should respect these capacities and the directions in which clients wish to apply them. Clients' motivation is increased by a consistent emphasis on strengths as they define them. The discovering of strengths requires a process of cooperative exploration. It turns therapists away from the temptation to judge or blame clients for their difficulties and toward discovering how clients have manage(d) to survive and maybe even thrive. All environments—even the most bleak—contain resources. Saleebey (2007) describes this as the *strengths perspective*.

SF questions for helping clients find strengths are:

- "Where did you find the strength to put words to what happened to you?"

- "How would you advise people to avoid such bad expe
- "When did you feel proud of yourself?"

Research done by Masten (2001) shows an important ⌣ between strengths and *resilience*. Strengths refer to attributes of a person, such as good coping abilities, or protective circumstances, such as a supportive partner. Resilience refers to the processes whereby these strengths enable adaptation during times of challenge. Thus, once therapists help clients identify their strengths, these strengths can be used to help them understand and enhance their resilience.

EXERCISE 15. SELF-APPRECIATION

Invite clients to think about the following:

1. "What are five things I like about myself?"
2. "What are five things I do that add value to the world around me?"
3. "What is my proudest achievement in the last 12 months?"

The present and future determine how we look at our past; it is said that it is never too late to have a happy childhood. Furman (1998) asked readers of two Finnish magazines who had endured difficult childhoods the following questions:

1. "What helped you survive your difficult childhood?"
2. "What have you learned from your difficult childhood?"
3. "In what way have you managed in later life to have the kind of experiences that you were deprived of as a child?"

The replies convinced him of the ability of people to survive almost any trauma. This gave him the belief that people can view their past—including even the most extreme suffering—as a source of strength rather than of weakness.

> Our past is a story we can tell ourselves in many different ways. By paying attention to methods that have helped us survive, we can start respecting ourselves and reminisce about our difficult past with feelings of pride rather than regret. (Furman, 1998, p. 56)

Asking these questions about how clients survived and what strengths and competencies they used may render exposure treatment unnecessary, as shown in the next case.

CASE 11. WHAT HELPED YOU SURVIVE?

The client says in a weary voice that, over the past 15 year, he has seen four therapists because of his depression. He has had psychoanalysis for three years, client-centered group therapy for two years, and extensive bodywork. Despite taking antidepressant medication, he is still suffering from depressive episodes. The therapist asks him the three questions as proposed by Furman (see Case 10). In answering the first question ("What helped you survive your difficult childhood?"), he answers that he has never thought of it this way. He has always seen himself as a complete victim of his abusive father, with no control whatsoever over the situation. He discovers that he actually *did* do something: He stayed away from home as long as possible and found a refuge with the parents of his school friend. He also realizes that his daydreaming ability (about how he would be a musician) has been a good strategy. The realization that he has actually achieved some things to escape his father transforms his vision of himself for the first time from that of a victim to that of a (partly) successful survivor. This change enhances his self-efficacy and generates further positive emotions.

The key to building a new habit is to practice the behavior, over and over. The famous aikido master Ueshiba states that instructors can impart only a small portion of the teachings and that only through ceaseless training can people acquire the necessary experience. His advice is to not chase after many techniques, but one by one to make each technique your own. This works for strengths as well. Here are a few ways that resonate for many clients:

y: Fill out the VIA (Values in Action) Survey of Character
ngths (www.authentichappiness.org) to find out what your signa-
e strengths are.

onversation: Talk with others about your strengths; tell stories about
how your strengths have helped you and were at play when you were at
your best. Use your strengths while you are in conversation; for example, if you want to build upon curiosity, ask questions with a sense of
genuine interest.

- *Journaling*: Write about your strengths; explore them in this intraper-
sonal way. For example, if you want to build upon prudence, consider
a situation you are conflicted about and write about the costs and benefits of both sides.

- *Self-monitoring*: Set up a tracking system to monitor your experiences
throughout the day. Track one or more of the strengths you are using
hour by hour; you might need an alarm or another external cue to
remind yourself to monitor when you use your strengths. This strategy
involves using your strength of self-regulation.

If clients cannot find any strengths, invite them to look at themselves
through a more positive lens. SF questions for helping clients to *find strengths
from a third-person perspective* are:

- "What would my best friend(s) say that my strengths are?"
- "What qualities and skills do they know I have?"
- "What would my kids/parents/colleagues say that my strengths are?"

- "When were others aware that I had those qualities?"
- "How will others notice that I use these qualities in this situation?"
- "What things are easy for me to do, while others may find them difficult?"
- "If . . . (e.g., a deceased person) could see how I am doing now, what will he or she be proud of?"
- "What would that person say about me, if that were possible?"
- "What would he or she say about how I have achieved this?"

CASE 12. LEFT AND RIGHT

The client with a long history of physical and sexual abuse finds it very difficult to name any strength. The therapist invites her to make a list of all the personal things she isn't happy about. These are written on the left side of a sheet of paper—after the therapist has drawn a vertical line down the middle. The therapist asks what she would like to see instead of each item on the left side, and when there are or were (small) exceptions to the problem. These are written on the right side of the paper. Then the therapist cuts the paper in half, and the left side is thrown into the wastepaper basket, which is the client's idea. From then onward, the therapist and client work with her goals and the exceptions to the problem.

EXERCISE 16. A RIVER CROSSED

Surviving a traumatic experience is like crossing a river: While fending for yourself, you develop new skills that can help you in the future. Invite clients to think about a painful experience that they have survived and answer the following questions:

- "What did I learn from surviving this experience?"
- "What strengths or talents did I draw on then or develop later to survive the experience?"
- "How can these strengths or talents be used to my best advantage now?"

EXERCISE 17. REFLECTED BEST SELF

Invite clients to ask 10 to 20 people to give them three written stories that describe how they made a contribution in some way. Ask them to collect all the stories and bring them together looking for common themes, surprises, and insights. Then ask them to synthesize the contributions into a *best self-portrait*, summarize their findings, and share the results with important people in their life. Twenty people may sound like a daunting number, but think of the impact this might have. Clients will have meaningful conversations with 20 people; they will solicit positive, engaging comments from these people; and they will probably connect with people across numerous domains of their life—personal, social, work, or spiritual.

Another way to find competence is through the technique of *competence transference*, in which clients are invited to talk about other areas of competence in their lives, such as sports, a hobby, or a special talent. Clients are then invited to bring those abilities to bear in order to reach their goals. As an example, a client suffering from a panic disorder learned to relax by applying his knowledge of breathing during deep-sea diving whenever he experienced anxiety.

CASE 13. COMPETENCE TRANSFERENCE

The client has for years suffered from the severe mood swings of her husband, a war veteran suffering from PTSD. She has tried everything but without success. As a horse trainer, she has a special talent for training supposedly untamable horses. When asked the secret of her success, she replies that she always rewards the horse for its achievements, even if the results are minimal. She also explains that she resists disciplining the horse or becoming angry and abandoning it. At that point she will stop for the day, offer the horse a sugar cube, and try again the next day. As she is describing this, she realizes that she could use her talent in precisely the same way when dealing with her husband's mood swings.

CASE 14. TREASURE BOX

When working as a Mental Health Trainer for Doctors without Borders or when working with children and their families, I often bring little sparkling treasure boxes. In these boxes, the trainees or children and their families keep all their competencies, strengths, and resources (and they may add new ones). The treasure boxes remain in plain sight, and I often refer to them during the training course or therapy.

Finding Exceptions

For clients, the problem is seen as primary and exceptions, if seen at all, are seen as secondary, whereas for SF therapists, exceptions are seen as primary. Interventions are meant to help clients make a similar inversion, which will lead to the development of a solution (De Shazer, 1991). When asked about exceptions, which are the keys to solutions, clients may start noticing them for the first time. Solutions are often built from unrecognized differences.

Wittgenstein (1953/1968) states that exceptions lie on the surface; you don't have to dig for them. However, clients tend to pass them over because they feel the problem *is always happening*. The aspects of things that are most important for us are hidden because of their simplicity and familiarity.

According to Wittgenstein, therapists shouldn't excavate, speculate, or complicate. That is why in SFBT, therapists stay on the surface and resist the temptation to categorize or to look for the *essence* of the problem. It is the task of therapists to help clients find these exceptions and to amplify them so that these exceptions start to make a difference for them. Heath and Heath (2010) call exceptions the *bright spots* (see Volume 1: Anxiety). Two types of exceptions are:

- *Exceptions pertaining to the goal*: "When do you already see glimpses of what you would like to be different in your life? When was the last time you noticed this? What was it like? What was different then?"
- *Exceptions pertaining to the problem*: "When was the problem less severe? When was the problem not there for a (short) period of time? When was there a moment you were able to cope a little bit better?"

STORY 13. SOLZHENITSYN

As a political dissident, Solzhenitsyn (1973) was for many years banished to a Russian labor camp. In discussing corruption of prisoners in the camps, he said he was not going to explain the cases of corruption. "Why would we worry about explaining why a house in subzero weather loses its warmth? What needs to be explained is why there are houses that retain their warmth even in subzero weather."

If exceptions are deliberate, clients can make them happen again. If exceptions are spontaneous, clients may discover more about them, for example, by monitoring exceptions or trying to predict them.

Therapists, having heard and explored these exceptions, compliment clients for all the things they have done. They invite clients to relate their success stories using three *competence questions*:

1. "How did you do that?"
2. "How did you decide to do that?"
3. "How did you manage to do that?"

The first question assumes that clients have done something and therefore supposes action, competence, and responsibility. The second question assumes that clients have taken an active decision, affording them the opportunity to write a new life story with influence on their own future. The third question invites clients to relate their successes.

Exceptions can be found in any symptom within the four clusters of the PTSD spectrum: reexperiencing the trauma, avoidance of stimuli associated with the trauma, negative cognitions and mood, and symptoms of increased arousal.

Some SF exceptions-finding questions in cases of PTSD are:

- "When was there a situation where you did not reexperience the event, although you expected you would?"

- "Which nights in the past few weeks were somewhat better (you slept better, had fewer nightmares)?"
- "When in the past week were you able to feel a bit more relaxed?"
- "When in the last few weeks did you not . . . (hurt yourself), even though you thought you would? How did you overcome the urge to . . . (use alcohol or drugs)?"
- "What happens when the problem ends or starts to end?"
- "When do you feel a bit more connected to others and the world?"

EXERCISE 18. PAY ATTENTION TO WHAT
YOU DO WHEN YOU OVERCOME THE URGE

Although clients often say that the problematic behavior (e.g., alcohol or drug use, gambling, self-mutilation, obsessive-compulsive behavior) always occurs, there are always circumstances under which the problematic behavior doesn't manifest itself (to the same degree). These are exceptions on which clients can build, because they are already part of their repertoire. This homework suggestion presupposes that clients definitely conquer the urge every now and then and that they are doing something different in order to overcome the urge. Clients' attention is directed to their behavior, not to any interior sensation. It may also be useful to draw attention to how other people overcome their urge in comparable situations.

CASE 15. BE GRATEFUL FOR WHAT YOU HAVE

Four years earlier the client lost her husband in a car accident. She was also severely wounded in the crash. Eighteen months ago her house went up in flames, containing her dog and many personal belongings. She was depressed and apathetic and sometimes thought about putting an end to her life. She could barely take care of her two children aged seven and nine, who spent most of their time with their grandmother who lived nearby. Her friends tried to cheer her up and distract her, but when she was back home the sadness fell over her like a blanket. Her family doctor referred her and prescribed antidepressants, which she soon stopped due to side effects.

The therapist listens to her story, acknowledging the impact of all the terrible events she has been through. Then she asks the client how she will know she doesn't have to come to therapy anymore. The client describes her desired life: She will be working as a secretary again and enjoying it (now she is on sick leave), her children will be living with her again, and she will perhaps have obtained a new dog from the animal shelter. The therapist asks how she manages to get through her days; how is it that she is still alive, and who has helped her so far? She says that her family, friends, and neighbors do their best to take care of her. The therapist asks, what positive things do those people see in her that make them willing to help her? Surprised, the client mentions that others find her an easygoing person, and that she has always been there for them when they needed someone. The therapist then invites her to write a *letter from her future* (see Exercise 9).

The next session she looks better, wearing makeup for the first time. She says she cried a lot while writing the letter and realized that she wanted to stay alive for her two children. A week later her children come to live with her again during the week, which leaves her the weekends free to go out with friends. She also takes the difficult step of going to the grave of her husband for the first time. Later she takes her children there too. After several sessions she is able to find meaning in life again, using her strengths, resources, and the help of significant others. The wise and compassionate advice she gave herself at the end of the letter from her future was: "Be grateful for what you have." It had become clear to her how grateful she was that her children had survived the fire. The therapist compliments her on her strengths, her progress, her discoveries, and her courage. In a follow-up session four months later, she says that she is doing fine and is organizing a dinner to thank her family, friends, and neighbors for their ongoing support.

Scaling Questions

By means of *scaling questions*, therapists help clients express complex, intuitive observations about their experiences and estimates of future possibilities. Scaling questions invite clients to put their observations, impressions, and predictions on a scale from 10 to 0 (see Volume 1: Anxiety for my reasons for using 10 to 0 instead of 0 to 10). Scaling questions may focus on progress, motivation, hope, and confidence. They can be asked at the end of the session, after one has looked for exceptions or discussed the miracle/goal. Scaling questions might go something like this: "If the miracle (or another description of the preferred future) equals 10 and the moment when things were at their worst (or you made the appointment) equals 0, where on that scale would you like to be? (For many clients, this is a 7 or 8). What will be different at that point? What else? Where are you now? How do you succeed in being at that point (how is it not lower than it is)? What will one point higher look? What will you be doing differently? How might you be able to move up one point? What or who might be helpful?" It is also useful to ask, "At what point do you think you can stop therapy?" or "On a scale of 10 to 0, where 10 equals you are handling what's happened very well and 0 equals you can't handle what's happened at all, where would you like to be?" Then ask all the follow-up scaling questions.

CASE 16. SCALING QUESTIONS

Say, "Here is a different kind of question, called a *scaling question*, which puts things on a scale from 10 till 0. Let's say 10 equals how your life will be when your best hopes are met and 0 equals the opposite (see Table 6.1.). Where on the scale would you like to be (X = realistic aim)? What will be different in your life then? What will you be doing differently? Where are you on that scale today (Y)? What is in that point (how is it not lower)? What else have you done? What will be small signs of progress ($Y + 1$)? What will one point higher on the scale look? How will you/others know you are one point higher? What will you be doing differently? Who or what can help you to reach that higher point?"

TABLE 6.1 Scaling Questions	
10	Best hopes are met
X	Realistic aim
Y + 1	Small signs of progress or one point higher on the scale
Y	Present situation and "What have you done to reach this point? How come it is not lower that it is? How did you do that? What does it say about you? Who would agree? What else have you done?"
0	Opposite of best hopes

STORY 14. AT THE CAR WASH

A car wash ran a promotion featuring loyalty cards. Every time customers bought a car wash, their card was stamped, and when they had eight stamps they got a free wash. Other customers got a different loyalty card. They needed to collect 10 stamps (rather than eight) to get a free car wash—but they were given a "head start": Two stamps had already been added.

The goal was the same: Buy eight additional car washes and then get a reward. But the psychology was different: In one case, you're 20% of the way toward the goal; in the other case you're starting from scratch. A few months later, 19% of the eight-stamp customers had earned a free wash, versus 34% of the head-start group (and the head-start group had earned the free wash faster; Cialdini, 1984).

So people find it more motivating to be partly finished with a longer journey than to be at the starting gate of a shorter one. To motivate action is to make people feel as though they're closer to the finish line than they might have thought (see Story 14). That is why SF therapists always ask, "How come the point on the scale is not lower than it is?"—thereby putting a few stamps on their clients' car wash cards.

From a cognitive perspective, depression, which often accompanies anxiety, is characterized by negative views of oneself, one's life experience (and the world in general), and one's future. In Volume 2: Depression, the focus is on developing a positive view of oneself.

Scaling questions are also frequently used in problem-focused therapies. However, these scales are about the problem: a depression scale, an anxiety scale, or an SUD (Subjective Units of Distress) scale in EMDR. On these scales, the highest point is where the problem is at its peak and the 0 is where the problem is absent. The absence of the problem doesn't say anything about the presence of positive feelings, thoughts, or behavior, as shown in the previous chapters. In SFBT, a neutral scale replaces an anxiety scale or stress scale, where 10 equals complete relaxation and 0 equals the opposite.

SF questions in this chapter are:

67. "Where did you find the strength to put words to what happened to you?" or "How would you advise people to avoid such bad experiences?" or "When did you feel proud of yourself?"

68. "What helped you survive your difficult childhood? What have you learned from your difficult childhood? In what way have you managed in later life to have the kind of experiences that you were deprived of as a child?"

69. "When do you see glimpses of what you want to be different in your life already? When was the last time you noticed this? What was it like? What was different then?"

70. "When was the problem less severe?" or "When was the problem not

there for a (short) period of time?" or "When was there a moment you were able to cope a little bit better?"

71. "How did you do that?" or "How did you decide to do that?" or "How did you manage to do that?"

72. "When was there a situation where you did not reexperience the event, although you expected you would?"

73. "Which nights in the past few weeks were somewhat better (you slept better, had fewer nightmares, etc.)?" or "When were you able to feel a bit more relaxed?"

74. "When in the last few weeks did you not . . . (hurt yourself), even though you thought you would? How did you overcome the urge to . . . (drink alcohol, use drugs, etc.)?"

75. "What happens when the problem ends or starts to end?"

76. "When do you feel a bit more connected to others and the world?"

77. "If the miracle (or another description of the desired life) equals 10 and the moment when things were at their worst (or the moment when you made the appointment) equals 0, where on that scale would you like to end? What will be different at that point? What else? Where are you now? How do you succeed in being at that point (how is it not lower)? What will one point higher look? What will you be doing differently? How might you be able to move up one point? What or who might be helpful? At what point do you think you can stop therapy?"

78. "On a scale of 10 to 0, where 10 equals you are handling what's hap-

pened very well and 0 equals you cannot handle what's happened at all, where would you like to be?" (and all the follow-up scaling questions).

In the next chapter, we will see how in follow-up sessions the focus is on small steps forward. When problems are large and overwhelming, taking small steps encompasses starting at a low threshold, low risk, bigger chances of success, and often a snowball effect leading to bigger changes.

7

Working on Progress

Introduction

In follow-up sessions, clients and therapists explore what has improved. The focus is on small steps forward. When problems are large and overwhelming, taking small steps is even more powerful than big leaps. Small steps ("baby steps") have the following advantages: a low threshold, low risk, greater chances of success, and a possible snowball effect enabling bigger changes.

Progress can also be made through inviting clients to rewrite their negative stories into more helpful and compassionate ones or through the use of positive imagery. Homework suggestions, intended to direct clients' attention to those aspects of their situation that are most useful in reaching their goal, may be added to enhance further progress.

Follow-Up Sessions

"What is better since we last met?" is an invaluable opening in follow-up sessions, even if clients have been attending for a long time. Ask for a detailed description of what is better, give compliments, and emphasize clients' input in finding solutions. At the end of the session, ask clients whether they think another session is useful, and if so, when they would want to return. In fact, in many cases clients think it is not necessary to return, or they schedule an appointment further into the future than is typical in other forms of psychotherapy.

According to De Shazer (1994), the goal of follow-up sessions is to ask questions about the time between sessions in such a way that clients can discern some progress. If one looks carefully, one can almost always find improvements. Another aim is to see whether clients think that what the therapist and client did in the previous session has been useful and has given them the sense that things are better. Follow-up sessions also serve to help clients find out what they are doing or what has happened that has led to improvements so that they know what to do more of. Other aims are to help clients work out whether things are going well enough that further sessions are not necessary and to ensure that therapists and clients do not do more of what doesn't work and seek a new approach instead.

Assessing Progress

How do therapists and clients know they are moving in the right direction?

Monitoring progress is essential and improves the chances of success. Duncan (2005, p. 183) states, "You don't really need the perfect approach as much as you need to know whether your plan is working—and if it is not, how to quickly adjust your strategy to maximize the possibility of improvement." Absence of early improvement decreases the chances of achieving what clients want to achieve. When no improvement occurs by the third session, progress is not likely to occur over the entire course of treatment. Moreover, people who didn't indicate that therapy was helping by the sixth session were likely to receive no benefit, despite the length of the therapy. The diagnosis and the type of therapy were not as important in predicting success as knowing whether the treatment was actually working. Clients whose therapists got feedback about their lack of progress were, at the conclusion of therapy, better off than 65% of those whose therapists didn't receive this information. Clients whose therapists had access to progress information were less likely to get worse with treatment and were twice as likely to achieve a clinically significant change.

The opening question "What is better?" suggests that some progress has been made and that one need only pay attention to what is better. This question is different from "Is anything better?" or "What went well?" or "How are you?" or "How have things been since our last session?" Clients usually react to this question with surprise. Sometimes clients initially respond by saying "Nothing," because that is what they experience from their point of view; they have not given any thought to anything better. In that case, therapists ask questions about the recent past and look for times when the problem was absent or less of a problem. Working on the assumption that one can always find exceptions if one looks for them, SF therapists ask questions not about *whether* there are exceptions but about *when* there are/ were exceptions. Alternatives to "What is better?" are "What is different?" or

"What have you been pleased to notice?" Therapists may also ask the four basic SF questions presented in Chapter 2.

De Jong and Berg (2002) developed the acronym *EARS* to distinguish the activities in follow-up sessions. *E* stands for *eliciting* (drawing out stories about progress and exceptions). *A* stands for *amplifying*. Clients are invited to describe the differences between the moment when the exception took place and problematic moments. Therapists and clients examine how the exception took place, and especially what role clients played in it. *R* stands for *reinforcing*. Therapists reinforce the successes and factors that have led to the exceptions through the exploration of these exceptions and by complimenting clients. *S* stands for *start again*: "What else is better?"

EXERCISE 19. WHAT IS BETTER?

Start the next follow-up sessions with "What is better?" Dare to ask that question! You will notice that clients start anticipating the next session and reflecting on what has improved. And if—unfortunately—the answer is that nothing is better or things are worse, first acknowledge clients' disappointment and find out how you can stay on a positive track with your clients.

Clients may provide *four different response patterns* to "What is better?" How well clients are doing and whether the homework suits them determines whether therapists should continue on the same path or should

ing else. Therapists should always tailor their questions and
suggestions to the alliance with each client (see Chapter 4). It
ant to keep in mind that clients want their problem solved, how-
simistic or skeptical they may be. For that reason, it is important
to listen closely and to examine *how* clients want to change. In follow-up
sessions, it is vital to optimize the alliance and to retain progress already
made and build on it. In addition, therapists need to verify whether the
homework has been useful, and any possible regression must be caught.
The four responses are (1) "Things are better," (2) "We disagree" (if there is
more than one client), (3) "Things are the same, and (4) Things are worse.
The good news is that for all four responses, SFBT strategies are available
(Bannink, 2010a, 2010c).

CASE 17. NOTHING IS BETTER

"Nothing is better" is the client's answer to the question about progress. The therapist invites the client to first tell her more about the
worst moment in the past week. After acknowledging this difficult
moment, the therapist switches to the question about exceptions:
"So the other moments must have been somewhat better. Please
tell me more about those moments. What was better about these
moments, and what exactly did you do to make these moments
happen?"

Clients who say that things are worse often have a long history of failure or have contended with big problems for years. If therapists are too optimistic, they will be unable to help them. These clients often need a lot of space to tell the story of the problem, including any (negative) experiences with previous therapists. More strategies for working with pessimistic clients are described in Volume 2: Depression. Suggestions to predict the next crisis and how to cope with suicidal feelings are described in Chapter 4.

Invite *clients who report that things are worse* to answer the following SF questions:

- "How do I manage to go on under these circumstances?"
- "How come I haven't given up by now?"
- "How come things aren't worse than they are?"
- "What is the smallest thing I could do to make a minimal difference?"
- "What can others do for me?"
- "What can I remember about what used to help that I could try again now?"
- "What would most help me climb back into the saddle and face these difficulties?"

EXERCISE 20. AT LEAST THREE COMPLIMENTS

tinually pay attention to what is working or what is different
J how clients make that happen. In every follow-up session, give
clients at least three compliments and ask competence questions:
"How did you do that?" "How were you able to do that?" "How did
you decide to do that?" (see Chapter 6). Take note of the difference
this makes for clients and for you as their therapist.

Gratitude

Gratitude counterbalances the aftereffects of trauma, because it changes
clients' focus from what is wrong to what is right in the world and in
their lives. The concept of gratitude involves more than an interpersonal
appreciation of other people's aid. It is part of a wider life orientation
toward noticing and appreciating the positive. This life orientation is
distinct from emotions such as optimism, hope, and trust. While these
emotions may arise from life orientations, those orientations do not
characteristically involve noticing and appreciating the positive in life.
For example, optimism represents a life orientation toward expectations, which involves future outcomes. Hope incorporates this focus as
well as the tendency to see ways through which these positive outcomes
may be reached.

Gratitude is strongly related to well-being (Wood, Froh, & Geraghty,

2010). Interventions to clinically increase gratitude are promising due to their strong explanatory power in understanding well-being and the potential for improving well-being through simple exercises (see below).

Research on gratitude (Seligman, 2002) shows that:

- Expressing gratitude has a short-time positive effect (several weeks) on happiness levels (up to a 25% increase). Those who are typically or habitually grateful are happier than those who aren't habitually grateful.
- People who note weekly the things they are grateful for increase their happiness levels 25% over people who note their complaints or who are just asked to note any events during the week.
- People who scored as severely depressed were instructed to recall and write down three good things that happened each day for 15 days. Clients were invited to set aside 10 minutes every night and write down three things that went well that day and why they went well. Ninety-four percent of them went from severely depressed to between mildly to moderately depressed during that time.

EXERCISE 21. GRATITUDE JOURNAL

Invite clients to buy a handsome blank book to be their *gratitude journal*. Ask them to describe the things for which they are grateful each day. Beyond simply listing good things in their life, ask them to describe why each good thing happened and what they have done to bring it about. Doing so draws their eye to the precursors of good events and their own strengths and resources.

EXERCISE 22. GRATITUDE IN FOUR STEPS

Invite clients to do this four-step exercise to increase their gratitude. By doing this exercise, they will experience more satisfaction and well-being. The four steps are as follows:

1. Find some ungrateful thoughts.
2. Formulate some grateful thoughts instead.
3. Replace your ungrateful thoughts with your grateful thoughts.
4. Translate the inner positive feeling into action: Do something with it.

EXERCISE 23. THINGS TO BE GRATEFUL FOR

Invite clients to note each morning, after waking up, at least 20 things for which they are *grateful*. This may seem daunting, but once they get into the habit and find the right frame of mind, it becomes easier.

Here are examples of things they could note and appreciate: "that I have running water," "that I have a roof over my head," "that I have clean clothes," "that I am alive," "that I have friends," and so forth.

Invite clients to discover what works best: writing down the appreciations, saying them out loud to their spouse or a family member, or silently noting them to themselves. Ask them to do this for a week and to notice what difference it makes. Then ask them to decide whether they would like to continue this habit or not.

CASE 18. ABLE TO BE GRATEFUL

The client told her therapist that she had eventually succeeded in putting the rape behind her. She remarked at one point that she was "grateful to be able to be grateful" for surviving and being able to enjoy the good things in life again.

EXERCISE 24. USE OF DRAWINGS

Invite clients to draw some happy events from their lives and ask them to explain them to you. Or ask clients to draw themselves while they are doing something they are proud of. Other ways in which drawing can be used include inviting clients to draw their preferred future, or to draw a circle and first point out where they would like to place the traumatic experience(s) in the future, where in the circle they would draw them now, and which steps they can take to decentralize their experience(s) (Bannink, 2014b).

Rewriting Negative Stories

Progress in psychotherapy can be made through inviting clients to *rewrite their negative stories into positive ones* or to use *positive imagery.* Once clients realize that they are not their story, they can start to develop stories or images that are more helpful and compassionate. There are four types of negative stories that can be challenged (O'Hanlon, 1999).

- *Blame stories*, in which someone is bad or wrong, has bad intentions, or gets the blame for the problem
- *Impossibility stories*, in which change is seen as impossible
- *Invalidation stories*, in which someone's feelings, desires, thoughts, or actions are seen as wrong or unacceptable
- *Unaccountability stories*, in which people are excused from responsibility for their actions by claiming that they are under the control of other people or some other factor that is beyond their control

EXERCISE 25. POSITIVE BLAME

As an example of changing negative stories to positive ones, this is an exercise for *positive blame*. Most clients talk about blame in a negative sense. They have probably never heard of the concept of positive blame and are surprised when the therapist asks what they are to blame for in a positive way. When therapists ask clients for exceptions to the problem, past successes, or present solutions, they are using a form of positive blame. How were you able to do that? How did you decide to do that? How did you come up with that great idea? The hidden message behind these *competence questions* is that clients have achieved a degree of capability and that, if appropriate, this success may be repeated.

EXERCISE 26. FIRST SMALL CHANGE
IN FEELING GUILTY

Invite clients who feel guilty to answer the following question: "You're feeling very guilty, but what do you think will be the first small change in your thinking that maybe, just maybe, it wasn't entirely your fault? That you did the best you could do in the circum- stance?" Or ask, "Could someone else have acted the same way?"

This is a useful question for helping clients to stop second-guessing or criticizing themselves for something that has happened.

CASE 19. FEBRUARY MAN

Erickson (1989) describes the story of Mary in *The February Man*. Using *hypnosis*, Mary was regressed to the age of six, when her little sister had climbed fully clothed into a bath filled with water. Mary had tried to pull her out, with the result that her sister had rolled under the water and nearly drowned. Mary shouted for her mother, who came running and grabbed the little girl, who was already turning blue. Mary felt still guilty and anxious when these memories were evoked.

With tears in her eyes, Mary told Erickson this story. Erickson started by affirming Mary's actions: "You saw that your sister was in danger, and you tried to get your mother to come to rescue her. You could not help losing your grip because you did not have enough strength to pull her out, but you acted cleverly in quickly calling your mother for help." Little Mary felt better as soon as she saw the incident with new eyes, and her *blame story* changed. Erickson used several of these kinds of encounters with Mary at different stages of her life, comforting her and sympathizing with her various painful childhood experiences.

CASE 20. IMAGINE THE SCENE AGAIN

The client is invited to use *positive imagery* in which she modifies a traumatic image to change associated negative thoughts, feelings, and/or behaviors. She says that she imagines the scene again, just as it occurs in her flashbacks. Only this time, her adult self goes right over to the little girl, picks her up, and takes her away, saying soothing, kind words and holding her gently but firmly close. Her adult self is protecting her from her aggressive mother. She says that this may sound crazy, but to her it feels great.

Yet another way for clients to deal with anxiety and fear is to become *amygdala whisperers* (see Volume 1: Anxiety). Amygdala activation takes place if traumatic experiences have produced maladaptive emotion regulation, restricting people in their ability to achieve emotional resilience and behavioral flexibility. This can be done by a number of self-talk strategies in which imagery or internal dialogue is activated.

Resilient people build a gentle relationship with their emotions and have a healthy way of relating to themselves: They go easy on themselves. Being kind to yourself is not only providing comfort in the moment; it is also committing, whenever possible, to reducing future instances of suffering.

Self-compassion revolves around three things, according to Neff (2011). The first is *self-compassion* instead of self-judgment. People who are kind to themselves are tolerant and loving toward themselves when faced with pain or failure, whereas self-judging people are tough and intolerant toward themselves. The second involves the notion of *common humanity* instead of that of isolation. Common humanity is a perspective that views failings and feelings of inadequacy as part of the human condition. People who isolate themselves tend to feel alone in their failure. The last is *emotional regulation* instead of over-identification. People who can regulate their emotions take a balanced view and keep their emotions in perspective. They neither ignore nor ruminate on elements of their lives that they dislike, whereas those who over-identify tend to obsess and fixate on failure and view it as evidence of personal inadequacy.

Increasing self-compassion creates positive effects such as satisfaction with one's own life, wisdom, optimism, curiosity, goal setting, social connectedness, personal responsibility, and emotional resilience.

CASE 21. A BIT OF SELF-COMPASSION

The client says that her youth was awful. Her parents, both psychiatric patients, treated each other and their children terribly. Later in life she and her own family suffered injuries from a plane crash, which they survived but which seriously wounded them. To add to this, at the time of the first session the client's youngest daughter had an unwanted pregnancy. The client explains that she cries a lot because she feels she is losing her usual perseverance and courage.

She finds it difficult to do nice things for herself and at one point wonders how she could become better at self-soothing.

The therapist acknowledges her feelings and normalizes the fact that she has difficulties in being kind to herself because her parents were never able to model this kind of behavior when she was a child. Without this model, how did she succeed in comforting her own children when they needed her? Where did she learn how to show compassion for others? The therapist also asks exception-finding questions: "When did you succeed in showing a little bit of self-compassion?" "What exactly did you do then?" "How can you do more of it in the future?"

EXERCISE 27. SELF-COMPASSION

Invite clients to think of moments in their life when they were able to be more kind to themselves, even just a little bit (exceptions). What exactly did they do? How were they able to do that? What were the positive consequences of these moments? Then ask them what small step(s) they may take to increase the prospect of more self-compassionate moments.

EXERCISE 28. LOVING-KINDNESS MEDITATION

Invite clients to find a place where they can sit comfortably without being disturbed. Ask them to rest their hands lightly on their lap, palms up, and to close their eyes and take a few deep breaths. Say, "Just let it be, and just continue to observe your breath. The goal in attending to your breath is to practice being present, here and now. There is no need to suppress your thoughts; just let them be and become aware of them as they come and fade away again."

Mindfulness exercises are used to cultivate *loving-kindness*. Invite clients to first reflect on a person (or animal) for whom they feel warm and compassionate feelings. Once these feelings take hold, creating positivity in them, ask them to gently let go of the image and simply hold the feeling. Then ask them to extend that feeling to themselves, cherishing themselves as deeply and purely as they would cherish their own newborn child. Next, ask them to radiate their warm and compassionate feelings to others, first to someone they know well, then gradually calling to mind other friends and family members and then all people with whom they are connected, even remotely. Ultimately, ask them to extend their feelings of love and kindness to all people and creatures of the earth: "May they all be happy" (Fredrickson, 2009).

EXERCISE 29. RAINY DAY LETTER

When clients need comfort, it is sometimes difficult for them to remember or figure out what will help. The *rainy day letter* (Dolan, 1998) provides consolation when clients most need it. They can carry the letter with them wherever they are. It offers wisdom from the individual who knows the person best: himself or herself. Invite clients to set aside some time when they are feeling calm and ask them to write this letter to themselves, including the following:

- List activities you find comforting.
- Record the names and phone numbers of supportive friends or family members.
- Remind yourself of your strengths and virtues.
- Remind yourself of your special talents, abilities, and interests.
- Remind yourself of your hopes for the future.
- Give yourself special advice or other reminders that are important to you.

EXERCISE 30. VICTIM OR SURVIVOR

There is a saying: *This is the first day of the rest of your life.* The following four-step exercise (Dolan, 1991) helps clients to find out which role they want to play in the rest of their lives, that of *victim* or *survivor* (or even *thriver*).

1. "How would you like to see your life in a month's time? The same people and circumstances are still present, but you feel a little less influenced by what you have experienced."

2. "If you think about your answer to the previous question, that is, your goal in a month's time, how will you then think and feel? How will you behave in order to reach your goal if you see yourself as a victim?"

3. "Answer the same question, but now from the perspective of a survivor or thriver."

4. "What differences do you notice? What will you be doing differently? Which attitude is the most helpful to you?"

EXERCISE 31. WORST CASE SCENARIO

If very pessimistic clients are expecting a visit or planning a holiday that they are dreading, ask them to pretend they are the director of a movie in which their family members are playing their usual parts (the ones that drive them or others crazy) and that their job is to get them to deliver their lines or do their usual behaviors to perfection.

> Or invite them to imagine some *worst case scenarios* before
> the visit/holiday takes place and compare what actually happens
> to those scenarios to see if they even come close (most of the time
> they don't).

Homework Suggestions

Many forms of psychotherapy consider homework to be important. However, De Shazer (1985) stated that he could get as much information when
clients didn't perform homework. He also found that accepting nonper-
formance as a message about clients' way of doing things (rather than as a
sign of *resistance*; see Chapter 5) allowed him to develop a cooperative relationship with clients that might not include homework. This was a shock
to him, because he had assumed that homework was necessary to achieve
behavioral change.

Nevertheless, at the end of each session, therapists may offer clients
homework suggestions intended to direct their attention to those aspects of
their experiences and situations that are most useful in reaching their goals.

Clients in a *customer-relationship* may get observation and behavior
suggestions (suggestions to actually do something different). Therapy with
these clients is often the

icing on the cake" and gives some much needed positive reinforcement
to therapists that they are competent.

In a *visitor-relationship*, no suggestions are given. After all, the problem has not yet been defined, nor is there any talk of a goal or related exceptions. Therapists go along with clients' worldview, extend acknowledgment, and compliment them on their personal strengths and resources and for coming to the therapist's office. They propose another appointment to continue to find out, with their client, what would be the best thing for them to do.

In a *complainant-relationship*, only observational suggestions are given. To clients who cannot name exceptions or a goal, therapists may give one of the following suggestions:

- "Pay attention to what happens in your life that gives you the idea that this problem can be solved."
- "Reflect on what you would like to accomplish with these sessions."
- "Pay attention to what is going well and should stay the same, or pay attention to what happens in your life that you would like to continue to happen."
- "Observe the positive moments in your life."
- "Pay attention to the times when things are going better."
- If scaling questions are used: "Observe when you are one point higher on the scale and what you and/or (significant) others are doing differently then."
- "Pay attention to what gives you hope that this problem can be solved."

The use of observation suggestions implies that exceptions may occur again and can contribute to clients' feeling more hopeful. These tasks also indicate that useful information can be found within clients' own realm of experience.

When clients are hesitant about change, therapists should suggest that they *observe* rather than *do* something. The thought of doing something may seem too big a step; an observational task may not seem as threatening. Since clients don't have the pressure to do anything different, they may be more likely to observe what they are already doing. By doing this, they will probably find more exceptions. If clients don't (yet) have any ideas about which step forward they might take, observation suggestions may be useful.

- "Observe between now and the next session when things are just a little bit better and what you did to make that happen."
- "Observe situations when the problem is there to a lesser extent, even just a little bit."
- "Observe situations where the problem is present and you can cope a bit better with it."

De Shazer (1988) sometimes adds an element of *prediction*. If there are exceptions, a *prediction task* suggests that they will occur again, maybe even sooner than clients imagine. If clients predict a better day, they will be more inclined to look for signs of confirmation (*positive self-fulfilling prophecy*). Clients in a complainant-relationship who can describe spontaneous exceptions may receive such a prediction task (see Exercise 32).

EXERCISE 32. PREDICTION SUGGESTION

Invite clients to:

- predict what tomorrow will be like, find an explanation for why the day turned out the way it did tomorrow evening, and then make a new prediction for the following day
- find out what contributed to the prediction's coming true or not coming true

CASE 22. FIRST SESSION FORMULA TASK

At the end of the first session, therapists give clients the *first session formula task.* "Between now and the next time we meet, I would like you to observe what happens in your life that you want to continue to happen." This intervention defines therapy as dealing with the present and the future rather than the past. The therapist expects something worthwhile to happen, and this is often the opposite of what clients expect to happen. This suggestion lets clients know that the therapist is confident that change will occur. This is an easy task for clients to cooperate with, since it doesn't call for anything different; only observations are required. This is something clients will do anyway, and this suggestion directs the focus of their observations.

As homework suggestions, invite clients to:

1. *Observe for positives*: "Between now and the next time we meet, notice what is happening in your life (marriage, family, work) that you would like to see continue" (*first session formula task*)
2. *Do more of the positives or exceptions* when these are deliberate and within their control: "Keep up what you are doing that is helpful and notice what other things you do that are helpful."
3. *Find out about spontaneous exceptions*: "Find out more about those times and what you do that contributes to those times being better."
4. *Do a small piece of the hypothetical solution*: "Experiment and just do a small piece of it."

CASE 23. AT LEAST 10 THINGS

The therapist gives the client, who is suffering from flashbacks and intrusive thoughts after having been severely wounded in a car accident, the following homework suggestion. "Observe at least 10 things that take you in the right direction [for the client, this means that he will be calm and able to think straight again] so that you can tell me about it next time we meet."

Should the client not be able to find these 10 things, he may ask his family members what they think is moving him in the right direction. Observing at least 10 things that work is challenging (and often fun) and ensures that clients will come up with more creative ideas than they probably thought they would.

Therapeutic Rituals

Performing *therapeutic rituals* can be one of the exercises therapists suggest as part of any homework. Rituals of various kinds are a feature of almost all known human societies. They include not only the worship rites of religions and cults, but also the rites of passage of certain societies, purification rites, oaths of allegiance, dedication ceremonies, coronations, marriages and funerals, school graduations, club meetings, sports events, veterans parades, and more. The performance of rituals creates a kind of theatrical frame around activities, symbols, and events that shape participants' experience and cognitive ordering of the world. This frame helps to simplify the chaos of life and imposes a more or less coherent system of categories of meaning onto it. Sometimes the healing of clients is inhibited by the lack of rituals to facilitate life cycle transitions. Therapeutic rituals can help clients mobilize their resources for healing, growth, and change. A therapeutic ritual can also help clients to resolve conflicts and resentments, to negotiate new roles and relational boundaries, and to develop new shared meanings about their ongoing life.

There are two types of rituals: rites of passage and rites of stability. *Rites of passage* mark a person's transition from one status to another, including birth, coming of age, marriage, and death. This ritual is specific and temporary and helps people because they are invited to become active instead of passively ruminating. Often a symbol is chosen related to the event, such as a photograph of the deceased or a piece of the car after the incident. During the therapeutic ritual, designed by clients and therapists together, this symbol is used—for example, by burning or burying it. *Rites of stability* often become a habit and are intended to prevent problems and obtain stability and connection after a traumatic experience. These rituals can be performed alone or together with important others and connect people in a positive way. Examples of stability rituals are writing in a diary or going for evening walks together.

EXERCISE 33. THERAPEUTIC RESOLVING LETTERS

To help clients to go beyond being survivors, Dolan's *therapeutic resolving letters* are useful (Dolan, 1991). There are four letters that clients write as homework and bring in to the next session. *Letter one* includes all the unresolved feelings that clients have toward someone or something that has happened. *Letter two* is the response that the clients fear getting, this being either a response from the attacker or someone who has no good intentions toward them. *Letter three* is the letter that clients hope they would get. It includes the acknowledgment they seek and, in the case of an attacker, also includes an apology. Letter three should be written straight after letter two in order to ease any trauma rather than deepen it. *Letter four* may be written at such a time as clients feel like writing it, and it represents the hope they have for a better future—a future in which the trauma is genuinely in the past and clients have gone beyond surviving it and have become *thrivers.*

EXERCISE 34. STABILITY RITUAL

Invite clients to think of a recurring activity that they used to do alone or with a partner/family member. Maybe they went to the movies together every week, read a book to each other, went out for an evening stroll, or massaged each other.

Given the current circumstances, ask them what ritual they could perform now. Ask them to invite the other person to participate and to check after one month whether this ritual is a good one for them and the others involved. If not, invite them to adjust the ritual so that it feels good, or to create another ritual together.

SF questions in this chapter are:

79. "What is better (since we last met)? What else is better?" or "What is different?" or "What have you been pleased to notice?"

80. "When did you succeed in showing a little bit of self-compassion? How can you do more of it in the future?"

81. "How would you like to see your life in a month's time? The same people and circumstances are still present, but you feel a little less influenced by what you have experienced. If you think about your answer to the previous question, that is, your goal in a month's time, how will you then think and feel, and how will you behave in order to reach your goal if you see yourself as a victim? Answer the same question, but now from the perspective of a survivor or thriver. What differences do you notice? What will you be doing differently? Which attitude is the most helpful to you?"

In the next chapter, we will see how SFBT ensures that clients are in the driver's seat. They decide when to conclude therapy. Behavior maintenance replaces the term *relapse prevention*, and suggestions are given on how to deal with impasses and failures in therapy. Right at the start of therapy, clients may be invited to think about how to celebrate successes, the conclusion of therapy, or victory over trauma.

8

Concluding Therapy

Introduction

Discussing the preferred future from the beginning of therapy generates optimism and hope. Clients indicate whether they think another session would be useful and when to end therapy. Instead of relapse prevention, SFBT pays attention to the progress made and how to maintain these positive changes. Also, four pathways to impasse and failure are described. Right at the start of therapy, clients are invited to think about how to celebrate successes or their victory over trauma.

Concluding Therapy

If therapists accept clients' statement of the problem at the start of treatment, by the same logic therapists should accept clients' declaration that they have sufficiently improved as a reason to end treatment (De Shazer, 1991). Each session is viewed as potentially the last, and sometimes just one session may be enough.

Contrary to traditional psychotherapies, discussion around ending therapy occurs as soon as therapy starts, as is evident from the questions about goal formulation: "What would indicate to you that you're doing well enough that you no longer have to come here?" In this way, therapists wish to elicit a description of what clients consider a successful result in positive, concrete, and measurable terms. A detailed description of the preferred future is key: "What exactly will you be doing differently that tells me that that's the situation you prefer?"

The moment when the sessions can be concluded may also be revealed by means of scaling questions: "At what point do you/important others/ the referrer think you should be on a scale of 10 to 0 in order not to have to come to therapy anymore?" Sometimes treatment can be concluded at a rather low point on the scale because clients have gained enough hope, confidence, and motivation that they can move toward the point where they would like to end up without therapy.

Behavior Maintenance

Relapse prevention is a standard intervention toward the end of therapy, but what are therapists actually suggesting or predicting when they talk about relapse? Of course, maintaining hard-won changes isn't easy, and clients have to work hard and show determination to do so. Instead of talking about relapses and how to prevent them, it is preferable to talk about the progress made and how to maintain these positive changes. In this vein, relapse prevention becomes *behavior maintenance.*

Focusing on what clients (and others) have done to help recovery or prevention in past experiences is useful. Therapists may map out a *recovery plan*—especially with clients who have severe mental problems like psychosis, major depression, or suicidal thoughts. This can usually be derived from asking about what happened as the client regained equilibrium after a previous crisis or hospitalization:

- "What were you doing when you started to feel better again?"
- "What usually happens when you begin to emerge from . . . (e.g., a depressive episode)?"
- "What did you learn from your previous crises/hospitalizations that may be helpful in this situation?"

EXERCISE 35. FIFTY WAYS TO
MAINTAIN POSITIVE CHANGE

Do you remember the song "Fifty Ways to Leave Your Lover" by Paul Simon? Making lists is often a fun and challenging task for clients:

- "Think of 50 *good reasons* to maintain the positive changes you made."
- "Think of 50 *ways* to maintain these positive changes."

■ "Think of 50 *positive consequences* (for yourself/important others) of maintaining these positive changes."

SF questions for *behavior maintenance* are:

■ "How do/did you manage to get back on the right track?"
■ "What does the right track look like? How did you/others notice you were on the right track again?"
■ "How did you find the courage to get back on the right track and not throw in the towel?"
■ "How do you know that you will have the strength and courage to get back on the right track?"
■ "How would you be able to do the same thing again?"
■ "What other qualities do you have that you can use to help yourself do that?"
■ "What can you do to ensure that you will maintain positive results?"
■ "On a scale of 10 to 0, where 10 equals great confidence and 0 equals no confidence at all, how much confidence do you have now?" (and all follow-up scaling questions).
■ "On a scale of 10 to 0, where 10 equals very motivated and 0 equals not motivated at all, how motivated are you to maintain your current success?"
■ "What can you remember and use from these sessions if a time comes when things are not going as well as they are now?"

Impasse and Failure

The average treated client is better off than about 80% of the untreated sample (Duncan, Miller, Wampold, & Hubble, 2010). But dropouts are a significant problem, and although many clients profit from therapy, many don't. Sometimes clients come back and say that things are worse instead of better, or that nothing has changed. This may be discouraging for therapists and clients alike, especially when everybody has worked hard. Clients also may feel embarrassed or ashamed at having to report failure or setbacks. The importance of *saving face* is discussed below. Moreover, even very effective clinicians seem to be poor at identifying deteriorating clients. Hannan et al. (2005) found that although therapists knew the purpose of their study, were familiar with the outcome measures, and were informed that the base rate was likely to be 8%, they accurately predicted deterioration in only one out of 40 clients! Duncan, Hubble, and Miller (1997) describe four pathways to impossibility: the anticipation of impossibility, therapists' traditions or conventions, persisting in an approach that isn't working, and neglect of clients' motivation (see Volume 1: Anxiety).

STORY 15. CLIENT WORSENING

Is it to be expected that clients will get worse before they get better? Of course not! Considerable clinical lore has built up around the idea that deterioration of the client's situation comes before the situation gets better. This is rarely the road to recovery and, in fact, is an indicator that portends a final negative outcome. This idea also allows therapists to ignore, to some degree, client worsening (Lambert & Ogles, 2004).

SF questions and tips for therapists for *solving impasses* are:

- "Does the client want to change (e.g., do I have a customer-relationship with this client)?"
- "What is the client's goal?"
- "Does the client have a goal and not a wish? Is the goal well defined and within the control of the client?"
- "Am I and the client looking for too much too fast?" If so, look for a smaller change.
- "Does the client not do the homework?" If so, provide some feedback to think about rather than an action-oriented task.
- "If I have gone through all the above steps, is there anything I need to do differently?" Sometimes we are too close to the trees to see the forest and may not recognize a nonproductive pattern between the client and us. A team or consultant may be helpful to provide a more detached frame of reference.

If a setback occurs, therapists should normalize it; progress often means taking three steps forward and one or two steps back (and it would be a shame to give up even a single step). Therapists may also give a positive slant to the setback; after all, a setback offers an opportunity to practice getting back on one's feet. If you fall on your face, at least you are heading in the right direction (O'Hanlon, 2000).

It is often not necessary to dwell on the cause of the relapse and its consequences. Therapists would do well to offer acknowledgment by showing that they understand how frustrating the relapse is to clients. Following this, it is important to explore how clients have managed on previous occasions to get back on the right track.

Clients (or their therapists) can also deal with relapse in a lighter, more playful manner: "What would it take for me to go back to square one as quickly as possible?" This immediately indicates what the wrong approach is and often lends the conversation a lighthearted tenor.

SF questions that may *create new openings* are:

- "What would be the best question I could ask you right now?"
- "If there were a last question you would like me to ask, what would it be?"

Berg and Steiner (2003) suggest the following questions for therapists to ask themselves if there is no progress:

- "If I were to ask my client how my contribution has helped, even if only a little bit, what would he or she respond?"
- "What does my client consider to be a sign of a successful outcome?"

- "How realistic is that outcome?"
- "What do I consider to be a sign of success?"
- "If my client's and my views differ, what needs to be done so that we can work on the same goal?"
- "On a scale of 0 to 10, where would my client say he or she is right now?"
- "What needs to happen to bring my client one point closer to 10?"
- "How much motivation, hope, or confidence do I have that this therapy will be successful? Supposing I had more motivation, hope, or confidence, what would I be doing differently? What difference would that make to my clients? How would they react differently?"

When clients feel overwhelmed and stuck, *saving face* is important. Clients are apt to experience their problems as impossible; seeking help offers the prospect of something better. Simultaneously, seeking help may also signify their failure to solve the problem on their own. Needing therapy can represent just one more unpleasant reminder of how badly they have managed their difficulties. If therapists suggest that the client's point of view is wrong, the alliance will deteriorate. What some colleagues call *resistance* may reflect the client's attempt to salvage a portion of self-respect. Some cases become impossible because the treatment allows clients no way of saving face or upholding dignity. This is what Erickson had in mind when he suggested that the art of therapy revolves around helping clients *to bow out of their symptoms gracefully*. He recognized that clients simultaneously hold a desire to change and a natural tendency to protect themselves if change compromises personal dignity.

Celebrating Success

At the start of therapy, therapists may ask already,: "How will you celebrate your success when you have reached your goal?" Children in particular find this a highly enjoyable way to start. A celebration gives clients closure on the goal they have been working toward, provides encouragement to continue, and makes every success even more worthwhile. The celebration doesn't have to be a big deal; it can be something clients do alone or share with others. It just has to make them feel good and help them enjoy their accomplishment. Suggestions for *celebrations* are described in Volume 2: Depression.

SF questions in this chapter are:

82. "What would indicate to you that you're doing well enough that you no longer have to come here? What exactly will you be doing differently that tells me that that's the situation you prefer? At what point do you/ important others/the referrer think you should be on a scale of 10 to 0 in order not to have to come to therapy anymore?"

83. "What were you doing when you started to feel better again? What usually happens when you begin to emerge from . . . (e.g., a depressive episode)?"

84. "What did you learn from your previous hospitalizations that may be helpful in this situation?"

85. "What would be the best question I could ask you now?" or "If there were a last question you would like me to ask, what would it be?"

86. "How did you manage to prevent relapse before?"

87. "How do/did you manage to get back on the right track? What does the right track look like? How did you/others notice you were on the right track again?"

88. "How did you find the courage to get back on the right track and not throw in the towel?" or "How do you know that you will have the strength and courage to get back on the right track (again)? What other qualities do you have that you can you use to help yourself do that?"

89. "What can you do to ensure that you maintain positive results? On a scale of 10 to 0, where 10 equals great confidence and 0 equals no confidence at all, how much confidence do you have at this moment that you can maintain these results? On a scale of 10 to 0, where 10 equals very motivated and 0 equals not motivated at all, how motivated are you to maintain your current success?"

90. "What can you remember and use from these sessions if a time comes when things are not going as well as they are now?"

91. "How did you succeed in staying away as long as you did?"

92. "What will it take to convince you that you are coping, even just a little bit, with all the difficulties that you are facing?"

93. "How will you celebrate your success when you have reached your goal?"

In the next chapter, we will see how therapists may improve their success by asking themselves reflective questions. Also, feedback from clients is essential for a successful outcome of therapy and for developing therapists' skills.

9

Reflection and Feedback

Introduction

Therapists should take the time to reflect on their contribution to the sessions so that they may continue to develop their skills. Furthermore, feedback from clients is essential and improves therapists' rate of success. Asking feedback invites clients to be full and equal partners in all aspects of therapy.

Reflecting on the Session

Research offers strong evidence that not all therapists perform equally well and that most therapists are poor judges of client deterioration. They are not good judges of their own performance either. Sapyta, Riemer, and Bickman (2005) asked clinicians of all types to rate their job performance from A to F. About 66% ranked themselves A or B. Not one therapist rated himself or herself as being below average! If you remember how the bell curve works, you know that this isn't logically possible.

In the case of a successful treatment, and in the case of stagnation or failure, therapists should look back on what they did. Reflection can be done individually or with colleagues in the form of peer supervision (Bannink, 2014c).

Reflecting questions for therapists are:

- "Supposing I were to conduct this session again, what would I do the same? What would I do differently?"
- "What would my client say I should do the same and/or differently?"
- "What difference will that make for him or her? And what difference will that make for me?"
- "Supposing I conducted sessions in the future with clients with comparable problems, which interventions would I use again and which wouldn't I?"
- "What positive aspects of this treatment stand out?"
- "What does my client want to achieve in meeting with me?"
- "How satisfied do I think my client is with my performance (on a scale of 10 to 0)? What would he or she say about how I managed to get to that point? What would it look like for him or her if I were one point higher on the scale?"
- "How satisfied am I with my performance (on a scale of 10 to 0)? How did I manage to get to that point? What will one point higher look like? What difference will that make for the treatment?"
- "Which of my client's strengths and competencies and features did or can I compliment him or her on?"

- "What strengths and competencies can my client utilize with regard to the problem that brings him or her here?"
- "Which strengths and resources did I fail to capitalize on?"
- "Which resources from the environment can help my client?"
- "What do I see in my client(s) that tells me that he/she/they can reach his/her/their goal?"

Clients' Feedback

Traditionally, the effectiveness of treatment has been left up to the judgment of the provider of this treatment. But proof of effectiveness emerges from clients' perception and experience as a full partner in the therapy process. Model and technique factors represent only 15% of outcome variance; they may or may not be useful in the client's circumstances. Therapists' theories should be deemphasized, and instead the focus should be on clients' theories. Exploring *their* ideas has several advantages:

- It puts clients center stage in the conversation.
- It enlists clients' participation.
- It ensures clients' positive experience of the professional.
- It structures the conversation and directs the change process.

It is clients who matter: their resources, participation, evaluation of the alliance, and perceptions of the problem and solutions. The therapist's techniques are helpful only if clients see them as relevant and credible.

SF questions for asking for clients' feedback are:

- "What feedback would you like to give me about today's session?"
- "What has been most useful to you today?"
- "What have you gained from this session?"
- "What had you hoped to gain from this session that you haven't? How can we remedy that?"
- "Before we end the session, can you tell me which questions have helped you and what questions you would have liked me to ask?"
- "What is the best or most valuable thing you've noticed about yourself today?"
- "What can you take from this session to reflect or work on in the coming period?"
- "What can you take from this session that can help you . . . (e.g., in the coming week)?"
- "What can you take from this session that will enable you to tell me that things are better next time?"
- "What difference has this session made for you?"

Using clients' feedback to inform their therapists invites clients to be full and equal partners in all aspects of therapy. Giving clients the perspective of the driver's seat instead of the back of the bus enables them to gain confidence that a positive outcome is down the road (Miller, Duncan, & Hubble, 1997).

Systematic assessment of clients' perceptions of progress and fit is important, allowing therapists to tailor therapy to clients' needs and characteristics.

In traditional psychotherapy, progress is measured by a decrease in problems, and usually therapists decide when to stop therapy. "Too often the client is willing to accept the absence of the complaint as 'goal enough,' but the absence can never be proved and, therefore, success or failure cannot be known by either therapist or client" (De Shazer, 1991, p. 158).

Progress should, therefore, be measured by an increase in the desired situation. Apart from *scaling questions* about progress, clients may fill out the Session Rating Scale (SRS) at the end of each session. The SRS is a feedback instrument, divided into the three areas that research has shown to be the qualities of change-producing relationships: (1) alliance, (2) goals and topics, and (3) approach or method (allegiance). The SRS is an engagement instrument: It opens space for the client's voice in regard to the therapy. The scale is aimed at starting a conversation to improve therapy for this particular client. Dropout rates are lower if the SRS is used. Information about the SRS can be found at www.scottdmiller.com.

SF questions in this chapter are:

94. "What feedback would you like to give me about today's session?"
95. "What difference has this session made for you? What has been most useful to you today? What have you gained from this session? What had you hoped to gain from this session that you haven't? How can we remedy that?"

96. "Before we end the session, can you tell me which questions have helped you and what questions you would have liked me to ask?"

97. "What is the best or most valuable thing you've noticed about yourself today?"

98. "What can you take from this session to reflect or work on in the coming period? What can you take from this session that can help you (e.g., in the coming week)? What can you take from this session that will enable you to tell me that things are going better next time?"

In the next chapter, we will focus on the well-being of clients; their partners, children, and friends; and, last but not least, their therapists.

10

Focus on Well-Being

Introduction

Reducing distress by making miserable people less miserable is just one side of our job; building success by helping clients to survive and thrive is the other side. The focus on mental health should be added to the focus on mental illness. Clients' well-being also concerns their partners, children, family members, and friends. Paying attention to what they are doing right, future possibilities, past successes, and their strengths and resources, instead of what is wrong with them and their relationships, generates hope and helps them in building on what works and what might constitute progress. SFBT also promotes therapists' well-being and reduces the risk of burnout. Therapy may be fun and empowering (again) for its therapists.

Clients' Well-Being

Our capacity to change is connected to our ability to see things differently. These shifts in perceptions and definitions of reality, which are a part of solutions-building, occur in conversations about better lives and useful exceptions. SF therapists don't empower clients or construct alternative meanings for them; only clients can do that for themselves.

Psychotherapy should not be the place where clients only repair problems and weaknesses, but first and foremost it should be a place where clients build solutions and strengths. Therapy should be aimed at increasing the well-being of our clients, at the same time ensuring that it will decrease psychopathology.

Trauma and Relationships

Trauma survivors may have trouble with their relationships or friendships. PTSD can cause problems with trust, closeness, communication, responsibility, assertiveness, and problem-solving. These problems may affect the way trauma survivors act with others. In turn, the way loved ones respond to them affects trauma survivors: A circular pattern may harm their relationships. Survivors often feel angry, tense or worried, distant from others, and numb. They may also have less interest in social or sexual activities. Because they often feel irritable, on guard, worried, or nervous, they may not be able to relax or be intimate. They may also feel an increased need to protect their loved ones and come across as tense or demanding. Trauma survivors often have memories or flashbacks of what happened and sometimes go to great lengths to avoid them. If they have trouble sleeping or have nightmares, both survivors and partners may not get enough rest. Survivors often struggle with intense anger and impulses. In order to suppress angry feelings and actions, they may avoid closeness. They may push away or find fault with loved ones and friends. Also, drinking and drug problems, used as a means to cope with PTSD, can destroy intimacy and friendships. Verbal or physical violence may occur. In other cases, survivors depend too much on their partners, children, family members, and friends. This dependency could also include those providing support, such as health care providers or therapists.

Partners, children, friends, or family members may feel hurt, cut off, or down because survivors have not been able to get over the trauma. Loved ones may become angry or distant toward the survivors or may feel pressured, tense, and controlled. The survivor's symptoms can make loved ones feel as if they are living in a war zone or in constant threat of danger. Living with someone who suffers from PTSD may lead the partner to have (some of) the same feelings of having been through trauma. Not surprisingly, social support may become more difficult if there is more than one person traumatized (in a family, group of refugees, group of soldiers).

As mentioned earlier, most trauma survivors don't develop PTSD. Also, many people with (symptoms of) PTSD don't have relationship problems. Relationships with others can offset feelings of being alone and help survivors' self-esteem. This helps reduce depression and guilt. Relationships can also give survivors a way to help someone else. Helping others reduces feelings of failure or feeling cut off from others. Last, relationships are often a source of support when coping with stress.

STORY 16. WE GOTTA GET OUT OF THIS PLACE

The favorite song of U.S. soldiers serving in the Vietnam war was a song by the Animals titled "We Gotta Get Out of This Place." The song was about the need to get out of the war because "Girl, there is a better life for me and you."

EXERCISE 36. SUPPORTERS

Much of what is positive in life takes place with others. Is there someone whom you feel comfortable phoning at four in the morning to tell your troubles to? If your answer is yes, you will likely live longer than someone whose answer is no. Isaacowitz, Vaillant, and Seligman (2003) discovered this fact in the *Grant study.* They found that the capacity to love and be loved was the single strength most clearly associated with subjective well-being at age 80. Invite clients to answer the following questions:

- "Who are my main supporters?"
- "How do they support me?"
- "What positive things would they say about me if I asked them?"
- "How do/did I support the people who support me?"
- "Which other people who have known me when I have not been

ill could remind me of my strengths and my accomplishments and that my life is worth living?"

EXERCISE 37. QUALITY TIME WITH FRIENDS

Positive relationships are important. To encourage clients to spend quality time with friends, invite them to answer these questions:

- "When did I last really catch up with my friends?"
- "When was the last time I engaged in activities with my friends?"
- "When was the last time I did something for my friends?"
- "What may help me to set aside more time for paying attention to my friends?"
- "What could I do to find (more) friends?"

STORY 17. IT IS NOT AN INSANE WORLD

"I want you to be able to talk to me about the war. It might help us to understand each other. Did you really kill seventeen men?"

"Yes."

"Do you want to talk about it now?"

"No. It's not that I want to and I'd rather think about the future.

About getting a new car and driving up to Vermont with you tomorrow."

"That will be fun. It's not an insane world. At least, our part of it doesn't have to be."

—SOURCE: WILSON, 1955

If *couples therapy* is needed, partners often come with a history of destructive and painful interactions, unable to work together to make the much-desired changes. It is important not to perpetuate this sense of failure, inadequacy, blame, and hopelessness by focusing on what the couple is doing wrong. Instead, a shift in focus to what they are doing right, future possibilities, past successes, and strengths and resources generates hope and helps couples in building on what works and what might constitute progress.

Ziegler and Hiller (2001) found that the best predictor of success is whether, early on, both partners begin to identify their individual and relationship strengths and become motivated to work together to bring about mutually desired changes. These changes take place if the couple turns into a *solution-building team*. As partners see themselves to be working as a solution-building team toward common goals, their hope, motivation, and effectiveness in making changes increases. And as they feel more hopeful about the future, they become more able to work collaboratively, both in therapy and in their everyday worlds.

Therapy starts by building a positive *alliance* with both partners. It is important to start building this alliance with the person who is more likely to be there involuntarily. Sometimes a partner is brought in for therapy because the other partner wants him or her to change.

SF opening questions about *strengths of the partner and the couple* are:

- "What is your partner good at?"
- "What do you appreciate in your partner?"
- "What do you like about him or her?"
- "What aspects of your partner are you proud of?"
- "What is positive about your relationship?"
- "How did you meet each other? What attracted you in him or her?" (*honeymoon talk*).

The process of clients complimenting each other by describing each other's strengths generates hopefulness and goodwill, which usually makes the rest of the session proceed in a more positive tone. Honeymoon talk (Elliot, 2012) is also useful because it changes the focus from problems to previous successes in the relationship.

Both partners are then invited to describe their best hopes for the relationship. In this way clients, can move away from past problems and frustrations and toward something more productive and satisfying: "What would you like to be different in your relationship?" "What difference will it make if the other person changes in the direction you want him or her to change?" "What will be different between the two of you?" "What will you be doing differently then?"

In couples therapy, partners sometimes want the other person to change, which puts them in a *complainant-relationship* (see Chapter 4). Clients often speak of what they don't want or what they want to eliminate from their lives. In interactional situations, they often speak of what they want their partner *not* to do. He or she is still in the dark as to what the other wants to happen. Talking about what clients *do* want may open up the conversation in a more positive direction.

Also ask about *exceptions*: "When is/was there a moment or a time when things between you are/were better, even just a little bit?" If clients cannot find exceptions, invite them to observe these moments in the time between the current session and the next. Also use *scaling questions*:

- "Where on the scale from 10 to 0 would you like to end up (what will be a realistic aim), where 10 equals your best hopes are met and 0 equals the opposite?"
- "At what point are you on the scale today (and why are you not lower)?"
- "How will you know you are one point higher on the scale? What will be different between the two of you? What will you be doing differently?"
- "At what point on the scale do you think therapy may end?"

CASE 24. ASK ABOUT EXCEPTIONS

One can distinguish between exceptions pertaining to the desired outcome (e.g., the preferred future of the couple) and exceptions pertaining to the problem. An example of interventions about exceptions pertaining to the goal is described below.

- *Ask about exceptions:* "So when your goal has been reached, one of the things that will be different is that you will talk to each other in a positive way at the dinner table. When do you see glimpses of that already? How is that different from what usually happens?"
- *Ask for details:* "When was the last time you talked in a positive way during dinner? What was it like? What did you talk about? How did you react?"
- *Give positive reinforcement (verbal and nonverbal):* "Was this new for the two of you? Did it surprise you that this happened?" Give compliments: "Where did you get the good idea to do it that way? What great ideas you have! Are you someone who often comes up with the right ideas at the right time?"
- *Project exceptions into the future:* "On a scale of 10 to 0, where 10 equals a very good chance and 0 means no chance at all, how do you both rate the chances of something like that happening again in the coming week (or month)? What will help to have that happen more often? What is the most important thing you

need to remember to make sure it has the best chance of happening again?"

CASE 25. RELATIONSHIP QUESTIONS

In couples therapy, both partners wish to restore their relationship. Their relationship has been under much stress since they both
returned a year ago from a tour of duty in Afghanistan. After some
honeymoon talk, the therapist asks *relationship questions*, in which
other perspectives are invited into the conversation (see Chapter 5).
Some of the questions from the other-position to the husband are:
"How will your wife be able to tell that as a couple you are starting
to get on the right track again?" "What will your wife say you will be
doing differently?" "What will your wife say with regard to how she
will react differently?"

Then the therapist asks the wife, "How will your husband be
able to tell that as a couple you are on the right track again?" "What
will your husband say you are doing differently then?" "What will
your husband say is helpful in making that happen?" The therapist
also asks both husband and wife questions from an observer position: "How will your two children be able to tell that things are better
between you?" "What will they see you doing differently together?"

Many of the *homework suggestions* described in Chapter 7 are also useful in couples therapy or family therapy. The suggestions are intended to direct the couple's or family's attention to those aspects of their experiences and situations that are most useful in reaching their goals.

EXERCISE 38. HOMEWORK FOR A COUPLE OR FAMILY

This is another *homework suggestion* for a couple or family: "This week I want you to observe at least two things you see the other person(s) doing to improve your relationship. Don't discuss this; just bring your observations to the next session."

The purpose of this suggestion is that clients start to observe positive interactions instead of negative ones and that they are more alert and willing to do positive things for the other person(s) now they know this will be observed and reported.

EXERCISE 39. STRENGTHS DATE

Planning a *strengths date* enhances a relationship and increases positive emotions for clients and their partners through understanding, recognizing, and celebrating one another's strengths. If the couple doesn't know their personal strengths yet, invite them to complete the VIA Inventory of Character Strengths (see www.

authentichappiness.org) first so that they know each other's top five strengths from this measure. Then invite them to take as many of their top strengths as they see fit and sculpt an activity together that taps into the individual strengths of both of them.

Therapists' Well-Being

Pope and Tabachnick (1994) found alarming facts about the work we do: Eleven percent to 61% of about 500 psychologists reported at least one episode of depression during their career, 29% had experienced suicidal feelings, and 4% had actually attempted suicide. In 2006, the American Psychological Association's Board of Professional Affairs' Advisory Committee on Colleague Assistance (ACCA) issued a report on distress and impairment in psychologists. They found that mental health practitioners are exposed to high levels of stress, burnout, substance abuse, and *vicarious traumatization*. Anyone in the (mental) health community knows about *compassion fatigue*. It is a condition characterized by a gradual lessening of compassion over time along with symptoms such as hopelessness, a decrease in experiences of pleasure, an increase in stress and anxiety, and a pervasive negative attitude. This has detrimental effects both professionally and personally, including a decrease in productivity, inability to focus, and development of feelings of incompetency and self-doubt. In the medical profession, this condition is called *burnout*. As stated earlier, exposure therapy is certainly not a *sine qua non* when working with trauma survivors. It is often exposure therapy that leads therapists eventually to experiencing burnout.

How can therapy be more kind, not only for its clients but also for its therapists? How can therapists prevent secondary traumatic stress (STS) and be resilient, or recover and even grow after STS? How can they survive and thrive and ensure *secondary posttraumatic success* (Bannink, 2014b)? It is about time to take better care of ourselves by paying attention to what we want to see expand in our clients and in ourselves. Many SF practitioners report that they have a lighter workload, more energy to spare at the end of the day, and, ultimately, less stress. Erickson (Rossi, 1980) states that if people emphasize what is positive, on the little movements that take place in a good direction, they are going to amplify these improvements, and this in turn will create more cooperation with other people (partners, children, friends, and colleagues). The same mechanism probably applies in client–therapist relationships.

STORY 18. WATER THE FLOWERS, NOT THE WEEDS

Peacock (2001)—author of *Water the Flowers, Not the Weeds*—told the following story. After a seminar that he gave to 250 managers, half of them bought a watering can. The managers put them, all different sizes and different styles, in plain sight in their offices to remind themselves that they were gardeners and that their job was to water what was working well in their organizations and in their personal life. Seligman (2011, p. 53) took watering flowers even more literally:

> I am a rose gardener. I spend a lot of time clearing away under-brush and then weeding. Weeds get in the way of roses; weeds are a disabling condition. But if you want to have roses, it is not nearly enough to clear and weed. You have to amend the soil with peat moss, plant a good rose, water it, and feed it nutrients. You have to supply the enabling conditions for flourishing.

EXERCISE 40. SUCCESSES IN WORKING WITH TRAUMA SURVIVORS

Interview your colleagues using these SF questions about *successes*:

- "When were you successful in working with trauma survivors?"
- "How exactly were you successful?"
- "Which of your competencies and strengths were helpful?"
- "What would your clients say you did that was helpful?"
- "On a scale from 10 to 0, how confident are you that this may happen again?"
- "What do you have to focus on to increase the chance that it will happen again?"
- "And what can you focus on to safeguard and maybe increase your own well-being in working with trauma survivors?"

Orlinsky and Ronnestad (2005) describe therapists at their best: They experience being personally engaged, communicate a high level of empathy, and feel effective and able to deal constructively with difficulties. It is about the therapists' sense of currently experienced professional growth and the feeling that they are learning from their day-to-day clinical work and deepening and enhancing their understanding in every session. This growth is fundamental to maintaining a positive work morale and clinical passion. Having this sense of currently experienced growth revitalizes therapists' morale and is their greatest ally against burnout.

Therapists (and their clients) usually experience SFBT as a satisfying form of therapy. Research shows that SFBT reduces the risk of *burnout* for those working in mental health care (Medina & Beyebach, 2014).

De Jong and Berg (2002, p. 322) describe the impact of SFBT on its therapists.

We spent hour upon hour listening to people's stories about what was wrong with their lives, and felt that in order to be effective, we needed to ask more and more questions about what was wrong. Solution-focused therapy was a breath of fresh air. All of a sudden, it was the client who determined when they were done with therapy. There were clear behavioral indicators when the goal was reached. We no longer had the burden of being an expert, but worked in collaboration with the client to figure out together what would be helpful. We no longer listened to months or problems, but were listening to strengths, competencies, and abilities. We no longer saw clients as DSM-labels but as incredible beings full of possibilities. Work became fun and felt empowering and our life outside of work was affected as well.

To develop a science of human flourishing and achieve the goal of complete mental health, *scientists* should study the etiology of and treatments associated with mental health and develop a science of mental health.

Until recently, the primary emphasis in the *training* of mental health was on pathology. Slowly but surely there has been a noticeable shift toward a more positive focus. In future training, we have to find a better balance between a focus on pathology and on repairing what doesn't work, and a focus on building strengths and resources and what works for our clients and their environment. Research shows that human strengths such as courage, optimism, interpersonal skills, hope, honesty, perseverance, and flow act as buffers against mental illness. Therefore, therapists should understand and learn how to foster these strengths in people.

The conversational skills used in SFBT to invite clients to build solutions are different from those used to diagnose and treat clients' problems. Many SF professionals and trainers believe that adequate therapeutic skills can be achieved with less training time and experience than is the case for other psychotherapies. Research on microanalysis (see Chapter 2) shows that positive talk leads to more positive talk, and negative talk leads to more negative talk. Thus, a therapist's use of positive content contributes to the co-construction of an overall positive session, whereas negative content does the reverse.

It is about time to take better care of ourselves as therapists by adopting a positive stance toward psychotherapy and by paying attention to what we want to see expand in our clients and in ourselves. There should also be a greater emphasis on outcome measurement instead of techniques of a particular therapy model. This change in the research and training of therapists will surely enhance the well-being of both clients and therapists.

SF questions in this chapter are:

99. "What is your partner good at? What do you appreciate in your partner? What do you like about him or her? What aspects of your partner are you proud of? What is positive about your relationship? How did you meet each other? What attracted you in him or her? What would you like to see different in your relationship? What difference will it make if the other person changes in the direction you want him or her to change? What will be different between the two of you? What will you be doing differently? When is/was there a moment or a time when things between the two of you are/were better, even just a little bit? Where on the scale from 10 to 0 would you like to end up (what will be a realistic goal), where 10 means your best hopes are met and 0 means the opposite? At what point are you on the scale today (and why are you not lower)? How will you know you are one point higher on the scale? What will be different between the two of you? What will you be doing differently? At what point on the scale do you think therapy may end?"

100. "So when your goal has been reached, one of the things that will be different is that you will talk to each other in a positive way at the dinner table. When do you see glimpses of that already? How is that different from what usually happens? When was the last time you and your husband talked in a positive way during dinner? What was it like? What did you talk about? How did you react? Was this new for the two of you? Did it surprise you that this happened?"

101. "Where did you get the good idea to do it that way? What great ideas you have! Are you someone who often comes up with the right ideas at the right time? On a scale of 10 to 0, where 10 means a very good chance and 0 means no chance at all, how do you both rate the chances of something like that happening again in the coming week (or month)? What will help to have that happen more often in the future? What is the most important thing you need to remember to make sure it has the best chance of happening again?"

References

Ai, A. L., Tice, T. N., Whitsett, D. D., Ishisaka, T., & Chim, M. (2007). Posttraumatic symptoms and growth of Kosovar war refugees: The influence of hope and cognitive coping. *Journal of Positive Psychology, 2*(1), 55–65.

American Psychiatric Association. (2013). *Diagnostic and statistical manual of mental disorders* (5th ed.). Arlington, VA: American Psychiatric Publishing.

American Psychological Association, Board of Professional Affairs, Advisory Committee on Colleague Assistance (ACCA). (2006, February). *Report on distress and impairment in psychologists.*

Arntz, A., & Weertman, A. (1999). Treatment of childhood memories: Theory and practice. *Behaviour Research and Therapy, 37,* 715–740.

Bakker, J. M., Bannink, F. P., & Macdonald, A. (2010). Solution-focused psychiatry. *The Psychiatrist, 34,* 297–300.

Bannink, F. P. (2007). Solution-focused brief therapy. *Journal of Contemporary Psychotherapy, 37*(2), 87–94.

Bannink, F. P. (2008a). Posttraumatic success: Solution-focused brief therapy. *Brief Treatment and Crisis Intervention*, 7, 1–11.

Bannink, F. P. (2008b). Solution-focused mediation. *Conflict Resolution Quarterly*, 25(2), 163–183.

Bannink, F. P. (2009a). *Positieve psychologie in de praktijk* [Positive psychology in practice]. Amsterdam: Hogrefe.

Bannink, F. P. (2009b). *Praxis der Losungs-fokussierte Mediation*. Stuttgart: Concadora Verlag.

Bannink, F. P. (2010a). *1001 solution-focused questions: Handbook for solution-focused interviewing*. New York, NY: Norton.

Bannink, F. P. (2010b). *Handbook of solution-focused conflict management*. Cambridge, MA: Hogrefe Publishers.

Bannink, F. P. (2010c). Oplossingsgericht leidinggeven [Solution-focused leadership]. Amsterdam: Pearson.

Bannink, F. P. (2012a). *Practicing positive CBT*. Oxford, UK: Wiley.

Bannink, F. P. (2012b). *Praxis der Positiven Psychologie*. Göttingen: Hogrefe Verlag.

Bannink, F. P. (2014a). Positive CBT: From reducing distress to building success. *Journal of Contemporary Psychotherapy*, 44(1), 1–8.

Bannink, F. P. (2014b). *Post-traumatic success: Positive psychology and solution-focused strategies to help clients survive and thrive*. New York, NY: Norton.

Bannink, F. P. (2014c). *Handbook of positive supervision*. Cambridge, MA: Hogrefe.

Bannink, F. P., & Jackson, P. Z. (2011). Positive psychology and solution focus: Looking at similarities and differences. *Interaction: The Journal of Solution Focus in Organisations*, 3(1), 8–20.

Bannink, F. P., & McCarthy, J. (2014). The solution-focused taxi. *Counseling Today*, 5.

Barrell, J. J., & Ryback, D. (2008). *Psychology of champions*. Westport, CT: Praeger.

Bavelas, J. B., Coates, L., & Johnson, T. (2000). Listeners as co-narrators. *Journal of Personality and Social Psychology, 79*, 941–952.

Beck, A. T., Weissman, A., Lester, D., & Trexles, L. (1974). The measurement of pessimism: The hopelessness scale. *Journal of Consulting and Clinical Psychology, 42*, 861–865.

Beck, J. S. (2011). *Cognitive behaviour therapy: Basics and beyond* (2nd ed.). New York, NY: Guilford.

Berg, I. K., & Steiner, T. (2003). *Children's solution work*. New York, NY: Norton.

Bohlmeijer, E., & Bannink, F.P. (2013). Posttraumatische groei [Posttraumatic growth]. In E. Bohlmeijer, L. Bolier, G. Westerhof, & J. Walburg (Eds.), *Handbook positieve psychologie* [Handbook of positive psychology]. Amsterdam: Boom.

Bonanno, G. A. (2004). Loss, trauma and human resilience. *American Psychologist, 59*(1), 20–28.

Brewin, C. R., Wheatley, J., Patel, T., Fearon, P., Hackmann, A., Wells, A., . . . Myers, S. (2009). Imagery rescripting as a brief stand-alone treatment for depressed patients with intrusive memories. *Behaviour Research and Therapy, 47*, 569–576.

Calhoun, L. G., & Tedeschi, R. G. (2000). Early posttraumatic intervention: Facilitating possibilities for growth. In D. Patton & C. Dunning (Eds.), *Posttraumatic stress intervention: Challenges, issues, and perspectives* (pp. 135–152). Springfield, IL: Charles C Thomas.

Carroll, L. (1865). *Alice's adventures in wonderland*. New York, NY: Appleton.

Charney, D. (2012). *Resilience lessons from our veterans* [Video]. Retrieved from http://www.youtube.com/watch?v=XoN1pv2JKpc

Cialdini, R. B. (1984). *Persuasion: The psychology of influence*. New York, NY: Collins.

De Jong, K. (2014). *Mass conflict and care in war affected areas*. Dissertation, Utrecht University, the Netherlands.

De Jong, P., & Berg, I. K. (2002). *Interviewing for solutions*. Belmont, CA: Thomson.

De Shazer, S. (1984). The death of resistance. *Family Process, 23*, 79-93.

De Shazer, S. (1985). *Keys to solution in brief therapy*. New York, NY: Norton.

De Shazer, S. (1988). *Clues: Investigation solutions in brief therapy*. New York, NY: Norton.

De Shazer, S. (1991). *Putting difference to work*. New York, NY: Norton.

De Shazer, S. (1994). *Words were originally magic*. New York, NY: Norton.

Doctor, J. N., Zoellner, L. A., & Feeny, N. C. (2011). Predictors of health-related quality-of-life utilities among persons with posttraumatic stress disorder. *Psychiatric Services, 62*, 272–277.

Dolan, Y. M. (1991). *Resolving sexual abuse*. New York, NY: Norton.

Dolan, Y. M. (1998). *One small step*. Watsonville, CA: Papier-Mache.

Duncan, B. L. (2005). *What's right with you: Debunking dysfunction and changing your life*. Deerfield Beach, FL: Health Communications.

Duncan, B. L. (2010). *On becoming a better therapist*. Washington DC: American Psychological Association.

Duncan, B. L., Hubble, M. A., & Miller, S. D. (1997). *Psychotherapy with "impossible" cases*. New York, NY: Norton.

Duncan, B. L., Miller, S. D., Wampold, B. E., & Hubble, M. A. (2010). *The heart and soul of change* (2nd ed.). American Psychological Association.

Dweck, C. S. (2006). *Mindset: The new psychology of success*. New York, NY: Random House.

Elliot, C. (2012). *Solution building in couples therapy*. New York, NY: Springer.

Erickson, M. (1954). Pseudo-orientation in time as a hypnotic procedure. *Journal of Clinical and Experimental Hypnosis, 2*, 261–283.

Erickson, M. (1989). *The February man.* New York, NY: Routledge.

Folkman, S., & Moskowitz, J. T. (2000). Positive affect and the other side of coping. *American Psychologist, 55*(6), 647–654.

Frank, J. D., & Frank, J. B. (1991). *Persuasion and healing* (3rd ed.). Baltimore, MD: Johns Hopkins University Press.

Frankl, V. E. (1963). *Man's search for meaning.* New York, NY: Vintage Books.

Franklin, C., Trepper, T. S., Gingerich, W. J., & McCollum, E. E. (2012). *Solution-focused brief therapy: A handbook of evidence based practice.* New York, NY: Oxford University Press.

Fredrickson, B. L. (2009). *Positivity.* New York, NY: Crown.

Furman, B. (1998). *It is never too late to have a happy childhood.* London, UK: BT Press.

George, E. (2010). *What about the past?* BRIEF forum.www.brief.org.uk

Gilbert, P. (2010). *Compassion-focused therapy.* New York, NY: Routledge.

Gingerich, W. J., & Peterson, L.T. (2013). Effectiveness of solution-focused brief therapy: A systematic qualitative review of controlled outcome studies. *Research on Social Work Practice.* doi: 10.1177/1049731512470859

Grant, A. M., & O'Connor, S. A. (2010). The differential effects of solution-focused and problem-focused coaching questions: A pilot study with implications for practice. *Industrial and Commercial Training, 42*(4), 102–111.

Haidt, J. (2006). *The happiness hypothesis: Putting ancient wisdom and philosophy to the test of modern science.* London, UK: Arrow Books.

Hayes, S. C., Strosahl, K. D., & Wilson, K. G. (2003). *Acceptance and commitment therapy: An experiential approach to behaviour change.* New York, NY: Guilford.

Hannan, C., Lambert, M. J., Harmon, C., Nielsen, S. L., Smart, D. W., Shimokawa, K., & Sutton, S. W. (2005). A lab test and algorithms for identifying clients at risk for treatment failure. *Journal of Clinical Psychology, 61*(2), 155–163.

Heath, C., & Heath, D. (2010). *Switch.* London, UK: Random House.

Henden, J. (2011). *Beating combat stress.* Oxford, UK: Wiley-Blackwell.

Horwitz, A. V., & Wakefield, J. C. (2007). *The loss of sadness: How psychiatry transformed normal sorrow into depressive disorder.* Oxford, UK: Oxford University Press.

Isaacowitz, D. M., Vaillant, G. E., & Seligman, M. E. P. (2003). Strengths and satisfaction across the adult lifespan. *International Journal of Ageing and Human Development, 57,* 181–201.

Isebaert, L. (2007). *Praktijkboek oplossingsgerichte cognitieve therapie* [Solution-focused cognitive therapy]. Utrecht: De Tijdstroom.

Joseph, S., & Linley, P.A. (2005). Positive adjustment to threatening events: An organismic valuing theory of growth through adversity. *Review of General Psychology, 9,* 262–280.

Jung, C. G. (1965). *Memories, dreams, reflections.* New York, NY: Random House.

Keyes, C. L. M., & Lopez, S. J. (2005). Toward a science of mental health. In C. R. Snyder & S. J. Lopez, *Handbook of positive psychology* (pp. 45–59). New York, NY: Oxford University Press.

Kessler, R. C., Sonnega, A., Bromet, E., Higher, M., & Nelson, C. B. (1995). Posttraumatic stress disorder in the national comorbidity survey. *Archives of General Psychiatry, 52,* 1048–1060.

King, L. A. (2001). The health benefits of writing about life goals. *Personality and Social Psychology Bulletin, 27,* 798–807.

Lambert, M. J., & Ogles, B. M. (2004). The efficacy and effectiveness of psychotherapy. In M. L. Lambert (Ed.), *Bergin and Garfield's handbook of psychotherapy and behaviour change* (5th ed., pp. 139–193). New York, NY: Wiley.

Linley, P. A., & Joseph, S. (2004). Positive change following trauma and adversity: A review. *Journal of Traumatic Stress, 17*(1), 11–21.

Macdonald, A. J. (2011). *Solution-focused therapy: Theory, research & practice* (2nd ed.). London, UK: SAGE.

Masten, A. S. (2001). Ordinary magic: Resilience processes in development. *American Psychologist, 56*, 227–238.

McFarlane, A. C., & Yehuda, R. (1996). Resilience, vulnerability, and the course of posttraumatic reactions. In B. van der Kolk, A. C. McFarlane, & L. Weisaeth (Eds.), *Traumatic stress: The effects of overwhelming experience on mind, body, and society.* New York, NY: Guilford.

McMillen, J. C., Smith, E. M., & Fisher, R. H. (1997). Perceived benefit and mental health after three types of disaster. *Journal of Consulting and Clinical Psychology, 65*(5), 733–739.

Medina, A., & Beyebach, M. (2014). The impact of solution-focused training on professionals' beliefs, practices and burnout of child protection workers in Tenerife Island. *Child Care in Practice, 20*(1), 7–26.

Miller, S. D., Duncan, B., & Hubble, M. A. (1997). *Escape from Babel: Toward a unifying language for psychotherapy practice.* New York, NY: Norton.

Neff, K. D. (2011). Self-compassion, self-esteem and well-being. *Social and Personality Psychology Compass, 5*(1), 1–12.

O'Hanlon, B. (1999). *Evolving possibilities.* Philadelphia, PA: Brunner/Mazel.

O'Hanlon, B. (2000). Do one thing different. New York, NY: Harper Collins.

O'Hanlon, B., & Bertolino, B. (1998). *Even from a broken web.* New York, NY: Wiley.

O'Hanlon, B., & Rowan, R. (2003). Solution oriented therapy for chronic and severe mental illness. New York, NY: Norton.

O'Leary, V. E., & Ickovics, J. R. (1995). Resilience and thriving in response to challenge: An opportunity for a paradigm shift in women's health. *Women's Health: Research on Gender, Behavior and Policy, 1,* 121–142.

Orlinsky, D., & Ronnestad, M. H. (2005). How psychotherapists develop: A study of therapeutic work and professional growth. Washington, DC: American Psychological Association.

Park, C. L., Cohen, L. H., & Murch, R. L. (1996). Assessment and prediction of stress-related growth. *Journal of Personality, 64*(1), 71–105.

Peacock, F. (2001). Water the flowers, not the weeds. Montreal, Quebec: Open Heart.

Pope, K. S., & Tabachnick, B. G. (1994). Therapists as patients: A national survey of psychologists' experiences, problems, and beliefs. *Professional Psychology: Research and Practice, 25,* 247–258.

Priebe, S., Omer, S., Giacco, D., & Slade, M. (2014). Resource-oriented therapeutic models in psychiatry: Conceptual review. *British Journal of Psychiatry, 204,* 256–261.

Rosen, S. (1991). *My voice will go with you: The teaching tales of Milton Erickson.* New York, NY: Norton.

Rossi, E. L. (Ed.). (1980). *The nature of hypnosis and suggestion by Milton Erickson* (collected papers). New York, NY: Irvington.

Saleebey, D. (Ed.). (2007). *The strengths perspective in social work practice.* Boston, MA: Allyn & Bacon.

Sapyta, J., Riemer, M., & Bickman, L. (2005). Feedback to clinicians: Theory, research and practice. *Journal of Clinical Psychology, 61*(2), 145–153.

Seligman, M. E. P. (2002). *Authentic happiness*. London, UK: Brealey.

Seligman, M. E. P. (2011). *Flourish*. New York, NY: Free Press.

Seneca. (2011). *Letters from a Stoic*. New York, NY: Seedbox Press.

Shapiro, F. (2001). *EMDR: Eye movement desensitization and reprocessing: Basic principles, protocols and procedures* (2nd ed.). New York, NY: Guilford.

Solzhenitsyn, A.I. (1973). *The Gulag Archipelago, 1918–1956*. New York, NY: Harper & Row.

Spitzer, R. L., & Wakefield, J. C. (2007). Saving PTSD from itself in DSM V. *Journal of Anxiety Disorders, 21*, 233–241.

Tedeschi, R. G., & Calhoun, L. (1999). Posttraumatic growth: A new perspective on psychotraumatology. *Psychiatric Times, 21*(4).

Vasquez, N., & Buehler, R. (2007). Seeing future success: Does imagery perspective influence achievement motivation? *Personality and Social Psychology Bulletin, 33*, 1392–1405.

Walter, J. L., & Peller, J. E. (1992). *Becoming solution-focused in brief therapy*. New York, NY: Brunner/Mazel.

Watzlawick, P., Weakland, J. H., & Fisch, R. (1974). *Change: Principles of problem formation and problem resolution*. New York, NY: Norton.

Weiner-Davis, M., de Shazer, S., & Gingerich, W. (1987). Using pretreatment change to construct a therapeutic solution: An exploratory study. *Journal of Marital and Family Therapy, 13*, 359–363.

White, M., & Epston, D. (1990). *Narrative means to therapeutic ends*. New York, NY: Norton.

Wilson, S. (1955). *The man in the gray flannel suit*. New York, NY: Four Walls Eight Windows.

Wittgenstein, L. (1968). *Philosophical investigations* (G. E. M. Anscombe, Trans.; 3rd ed.). New York, NY: Macmillan. (Original work published 1953)

Wood, A. M., Froh, J. J., & Geraghty, A. W. A. (2010). Gratitude and well-being: A review and theoretical integration. *Clinical Psychology Review*, in press.

Ziegler, P., & Hiller, T. (2001). *Recreating partnership*. New York, NY: Norton.

Websites

Association for the Quality Development of Solution-Focused Consulting and Training (SFCT): www.asfct.org

Bannink, Fredrike (author of this book): www.fredrikebannink.com

BRIEF, Centre for Solution-Focused Practice, London: www.brief.org.uk

Brief Family Therapy Center, Milwaukee, WI: www.brief-therapy.org

Centre for Solutions Focus at Work: www.sfwork.com

European Brief Therapy Association (EBTA): www.ebta.nu

Gingerich, Wally (with SFBT research): www.gingerich.net

Heart and Soul of Change Project (Barry L. Duncan): www.heartandsoulofchange.com

Institute for Solution-Focused Therapy (Yvonne Dolan): www.solutionfocused.net

Macdonald, Alasdair (with SF research): www.solutionsdoc.co.uk

Miller, Scott D. (with the Outcome Rating Scale and Session Rating Scale): www.scottdmiller.com

O'Hanlon, Bill (author): www.billohanlon.com

Reteaming (Ben Furman): www.reteaming.com

Solution-Focused Brief Therapy Association (SFBTA): www.sfbta.org

Solutions in Organisations Link: www.solworld.org

University of Pennsylvania, Authentic Happiness (Seligman with positive psychology questionnaires): www.authentichappiness.org

Index

Note: Italicized page locators indicate figures; tables are noted with *t*.

About the Author

Fredrike Bannink is a clinical psychologist and a Master of Dispute Resolution based in Amsterdam. She is an internationally recognized keynote presenter and provides training courses all over the world. She is also a Mental Health Trainer for Doctors Without Borders.

Dr. Bannink is the author of 25+ books on SF interviewing, SF mediation/conflict management, SF leadership, positive CBT, positive psychology, positive supervision, and posttraumatic success.

www.fredrikebannink.com